What Experts Say About The Mentor

We need caring, interested, and compassionate educators as found in *The Mentor*, a book that is filled with empowering lessons learned through creative new models for education. Bravo!

Dr. Charles Patterson,
Former ASCD President and Texas Superintendent

The Mentor is a creative teaching tool for educators and administrators in school districts who wish to broaden their horizons and embrace change from their highest and most loving selves. The candid dialogue that Hannah has with her staff shows that being direct in the name of serving a higher purpose trumps the typical "feel good" approach. Teared up at moments of mutual respect.

Tobye Adar,
International Author and Playwright, Tel Aviv, Israel

WOW! So powerful, so thought provoking, and so confirming! It teaches without lecturing. What a great book for beginning principals/leaders and even for old experienced ones (like myself)! I see some part of myself in Principal Hannah, especially when she has to stand alone on her principles. Congratulations.

Alice Reh, New York State Principal

From a leadership perspective, *The Mentor* is an example of change, highlighting the thoughts of a transformational leader. Written in an informal style, interactions bridge generations of stakeholders to demonstrate ethical standards in mentoring.

Dr. Gale Sookdeo,
NYC National Board Certified Teacher and Mentor

Whenever I have a difficult meeting to run, I reread *The Mentor* to find my center. After reading a poignant passage or two, I feel refreshed and ready to lead with love.

Ruth Gafni, New Jersey Headmaster

Just finished reading *The Mentor* and LOVED it! It is the story of many leaders, fused with spirituality and love for clients and our profession. I wished I were given a book like this early on, as it rings truth.

Mary Gomez, Dulce New Mexico Reservation Teacher

The ideals presented in *The Mentor* apply not only to those in the field of education, but also to the business world in general. It is a must read for all who wish to build their leadership capacity amid the dramatic challenges of change.

Myrna Loiterstein, Business Owner, Boca Raton, FL

THE MENTOR

Leading with Love: The Ultimate Resource

Jan Hammond and Rita Senor

iUniverse LLC
Bloomington

THE MENTOR

iUniverse books may be ordered through booksellers or by contacting:

iUniverse
1663 Liberty Drive
Bloomington, IN 47403
www.iuniverse.com
1-800-Authors (1-800-288-4677)

EDU 032000: Education Leadership
BUS 071000: Business Leadership
BUS 106000: Mentoring and Coaching

ISBN: 978-1-4917-0850-7 (e)
ISBN: 978-1-4917-0849-1 (hc)
ISBN: 978-1-4917-0848-4 (sc)

Library of Congress Control Number: 2013916850

Printed in the United States of America.
iUniverse rev. date: 11/26/13

This book is dedicated to all mentors: past, present, and future.

The Mentor

Chapter 3: November

Chapter 4: December

Chapter 5: January

Chapter 6: February

Chapter 7: March

Chapter 8: April

Chapter 9: May

Acknowledgements

As professors and practitioners of educational administration, originally we were going to write a textbook to crystalize the research in organizational leadership for practitioners that is critical for leading schools in the 21ˢᵗ century. Then, because we know the power of story, as in *Gung Ho!* (Blanchard & Bowles, 1998), we had the idea of writing theory on one page of the book and a story on how the theory can be put into practice on the other side of the page.

However, at some point, the story became more poignant than the theoretical overview. So, we scratched the academic writing of the theory; rather, we incorporated the theory into the story. Voila! The birth of "The Mentor."

Thank You to the Authors and Researchers. With that understanding, our thankfulness begins with sincere thanks to all of the researchers and authors over the last century whose contributions to organizational theory have paved the way for leaders who truly desire to lead ethically with head, heart, and spirit. We have included a reference section that highlights some of the outstanding theorists who have made their mark in our field. Because of space concerns, we did not include all, even though, if you read carefully, you will be able to find additional theories. A special thanks to the writings of Ken Blanchard, Lee Bolman, John Cross, Terrance Deal, Peter Drucker, Neville Goddard, Jennifer James, Kurt Lewin, Florence Scovel Shinn, Lao Tzu, and Wallace D. Wattles.

Thank You to Our Mentors. We want to thank those who have been exceptional mentors to us over the years. Special thanks goes to superintendents Dr. Herbert Fliegner (Tuxedo Union Free School District), Dr. Frank Eckelt (Lakeland Schools and State University of New York), Dr. James Vaccaro (Phoenix Central Schools) and Dr. Stanley Toll (Ardsley Union Free School District). Also, great thanks goes to principals Mark Montoney (Phoenix Middle School), William Zeralsky (North Salem High School), professors Dr. Red Owl (Long Island University), Dr. Frank Smith (Teachers College, Columbia University), Dr. Raghavan Parthasarthy (CUNY Baruch College, Zicklin School of Business), Karen Ranung (Curtiss School of Music), Dr. Lewis Baldwin (OCC and Syracuse University), and Dr. Rose Rudnitski (SUNY New Paltz and Dean of Felician College); and College President Steven Poskanzer (Carleton College).

Thank You to Those Who Read Our Drafts. We are especially grateful for those who took the time to read our drafts. Hats off to Myrna Loiterstein (business owner, Boca Raton, FL), Ruth Gafni (headmaster of Solomon Schechter, NJ), Dr. Charles Patterson (superintendent of Killeen Independent School District, TX), Dr. Lloyd Jaeger (superintendent of Millbrook Central Schools, NY), Alice Reh (principal of Otisville Elementary, NY), Dr. Tracy Hammond (Computer Science professor, Texas A&M), Rev. Dr. Marshall Cook (First Congregational Church, Ft. Pierce, FL), Dr. Gale Sookdeo (NYC National Board Certified teacher and mentor), Mary Gomez (first grade teacher on the Dulce, NM Indian Reservation), Connie Barnett (opera singer/coach, NYC), Tobye Adar (international author/playwright, Israel), and the iUniverse editorial team, with special recognition for Adalee Cooney and Kathi Wittkamper.

Thank You to Those Who Are Special in Our Lives. No one writes a book that takes nearly a decade to come to fruition without the support of family and friends. Jan is eternally grateful to her parents: Rod and Jayne Hammond, and Vedavalli and S. Raghavan Iyengar; and to Jan's husband, Dr. Raghavan Parthasarthy and their children: Madhavan Parthasarthy and his wife, Jen, and Tracy Hammond, with each one modeling the highest ethical standards. Jan also wants to thank her colleagues and the students in her life who have brought joy into the classrooms from K-12 and throughout the doctoral level.

Rita gives love and great thanks to her parents. Though her dad died at her young age of 10, she still remembers his leadership as a tugboat captain on the Hudson River, always appreciating the spiritual side of life. Rita's mom, also named Rita, lived to nearly age 95, continually showing Rita and the world the ethical path, living each day graciously. Rita has an extended family of friends who also deserve special recognition for their outstanding support throughout this journey: Edward and Maryanne Baxter, Donna DiDonna, Joan Moselle, and Janet Wood. Rita is also grateful for her students from ages 3-65, each giving a unique perspective on mentoring and learning through the joy of discovery.

Conclusion. Yes, if you haven't guessed it, this book is really a book on how to lead ethically with love, truly caring about the unique individuals who need your vision to guide them as they work toward achieving the organizational mission. And, yes, it is each leader's job to mentor the next generation of leaders who will make this a better world in which to live.

Jan Hammond, Ed. D.   Rita Senor, MA, CAS

THE MENTOR

LEADING WITH LOVE:
THE ULTIMATE RESOURCE

Now You Know Everything About This Book

Chapter 1: September

1
Awakening the Leader Within

AT 6:50 A.M. ON A brisk, sunny September morning, Hannah Gardner pulls into the middle school parking lot and parks her Ford SUV hybrid in the spot marked "Principal." She feels her heart jump with excitement, as first-day-of-school memories flash through her mind.

She pulls out her briefcase from the back seat and gathers two vases of fresh flowers and straightens her well-tailored navy blue suit. As she closes the car door, she catches sight of the first teacher rolling in. *Looks like Ms. Joyner,* thinks Hannah, raising her hand to say, "hi." At that moment Hannah's air of excitement turns to an unsettled feeling of doubt, questioning her own efficacy, despite the wave back from her music teacher. Taking a deep breath, Hannah ignores her opening day jitters and heads toward the Main Office.

It is one hour and fifteen minutes prior to the start of school. Hannah inserts the office key to unlock the main doors. Darci, her main office secretary, is not expected for another twenty minutes. Hannah finds her second key, and, as she opens the door to her private office, she takes a moment to gaze at her workplace. The room glows with the sun's rays on the attractive décor, accenting her well-organized bookshelves, pictures of former students, and other school memorabilia. She values the transformation from the starkness of three weeks ago when she was first hired and introduced to the sterile environment, compared to now, a warm inviting atmosphere.

Hannah sets her briefcase and the vases on her desk and sits down for a moment to contemplate. Appreciating the smell of the fresh flowers, a wave of sweetness settles her. *Start with what you know*, as her thoughts wander back as to why she accepted this position in the first place. She opens her briefcase and reviews her *to do* list. "Let's see, review morning announcements with the secretary, make sure all faculty have student handbooks, meet the buses at 8:30 a.m., and cabinet meeting with the superintendent at 10:30 a.m. Well, that should get me to the lunch hour," Hannah says out loud, laughing at her over-zealousness.

Hannah picks up one of the flowering vases and sets it on her secretary's desk. Down the hall she hears Frank Amber, the beloved custodian, known for his high ethics, whistling, "When the Saints Go Marching In," as he pushes his broom from side to side. The friendly tune draws her to the door and she greets the lean custodian with, "Nice music, Frank."

Dressed in a crisp white shirt, grey pants, and shined shoes, his eyes sparkle as he nods to Hannah and continues whistling.

The serenity of the melodic sound is shattered when the main door is thrown open, slamming into the side of the building. Darci Caldwell, the principal's secretary and known for her curtness, mumbles to herself, complaining about the lines in the parking lot. "Who the heck changed the parking spots? Mine isn't where it's supposed to be!"

As soon as Darci gets to her desk, the phone starts ringing. Grumbling to herself, she puts her designer bag down, pushes aside the flower vase, and grabs the phone, chipping a nail. "Summitville Middle School, good morning!" Darci barks, looking down at her French manicure. "Yes, uh--huh, no. No, that's not the way things are done around here. There is no school lunch credit. Your child will have to go without lunch today. That's right!" she commands, as she hangs up the phone.

Overhearing her secretary's abrasive words, Hannah instantly knows that her day is not going to be driven only by her organized *to do* list.

2

McCloud Over Summitville

IN HER INTERVIEW WITH THE superintendent, Hannah has learned that Mr. Gerald McCloud has been superintendent for the Summitville Central School District for the past 12 years. He had been a physical education teacher, a winning coach, and a mainstay in Summitville, entwined in local politics for the last thirty-two years. It is commonly known that he and his board run the town. Although sometimes their actions are less than admirable and can often be construed as downright trickery, few members of the town have ever confronted him and his board in public.

When Hannah gets to the district office at 10:25 a.m., she passes by Coach Tom Riley dressed in his uniform of sweats, sneakers, and his old lettered jacket rushing out of the superintendent's office. She finds Mr. McCloud on the phone in an active conversation, twisting his high school class ring on his finger.

A belly laugh cuts through the air. "Ha-ha, that's right, Judge. None of our buses can make it down your private road. Besides, I wouldn't want to have any of our buses shot at, just in case you were downing that imported liquor I got you last Christmas and thought it was a big moose!" The belly laugh is echoed around the room.

The superintendent's hand, adorned by a gold watch, motions Hannah into the room. She looks around the superintendent's wooden conference table and sees the other principals and the business administrator already seated near their boss. Taking the last seat in the room, she quickly surmises that she is late, even though she is on time for the 10:30 a.m. meeting and learns her first unwritten rule: *Get to the meeting early to get a premier seat.*

Once off the phone, the superintendent relaxes and says, "Gentlemen, oh, ah, excuse me, and lady, as you know, our newly-elected board met last night and gave me the following targets." He passes out the two-page document to each administrator. "We're all here today to implement these goals, school by school. You know, guys, my evaluation is measured by reaching these goals—which, in reality, are the test scores." Looking directly at the business administrator he says, "Oh, and, may I add, how well we are able to keep taxes down." His raucous laugh makes the table shake. "And, if my evaluation is measured by the accomplishment of these district goals, guess how each of your evaluations will be measured," he cajoles, as he leans back in his chair with a big grin on his face.

Hannah freezes for a moment. She hadn't given any thought to a formal evaluation as an administrator. With her former principal, she was evaluated as part of the administrative team, so the evaluations were always in tandem, always involved open and honest conversation, and were never a surprise. She remembers the times as a teacher when she was evaluated. She still remembers the panic she felt whenever the administrator came into her classroom, despite the fact that Hannah was considered an excellent teacher. How is this superintendent going to observe her? When will it happen? She quickly learns a second rule: *Her evaluation will be based on someone else's agenda.*

She regains focus when she overhears the superintendent state that the performance of the students in the middle school is this year's target. "Of course," laughs the superintendent, "this has nothing to do with the fact that six of the seven board members have children or grandchildren in grades 5-8!" as he shoots a penetrating look toward her.

Bob Walton, the heavy-set, seasoned high school principal, with a worn look on his lined face, addresses the statement. He looks at the superintendent, and, with a frequent glance toward Hannah, says, "I find that each new class that comes into the high school seems to have more problems than the previous class: students are less disciplined, more selfish, more into their own social cliques, more disrespectful of each other, and, of their teachers and adults. Their language and attitudes mirror their media viewing. These students have no appreciation of the free education that is being given to them. Their mobile devices are their lifeline; they are constantly texting each other. The English teachers are crying because they say that these kids can't even spell or write."

"I don't understand," argues Carl Evans, the jovial elementary principal, as he unbuttons his grey sweater, feeling the heat in the room. "We made sure that they got a good foundation in the elementary school—just look at our test scores. What happened along the way?" he banters back, as his eyes catch Hannah's concerned look.

By the end of the meeting, Hannah awakens to the fact that she is in a tenuous position, at best. She thought that becoming a school leader was about supporting the development of future quality citizens, not about test scores. Experiencing a bit of a culture shock from what she once knew as an environment dominated by nurturing energy when she was an assistant principal and teacher; she now recognizes that she's part of a select few who work from a left-brain dominated decision-making mode.

Hannah gets up from her chair, feeling a bit disenchanted. Tim Dowling, the respected business administrator, takes off his glasses and whispers to her, "Don't take it personally. There are growing pains with every new job. Just keep your smile—you'll do fine."

Hannah nods in appreciation. Before leaving, she opens her notebook and quickly writes: *A simple act of kindness goes a long way.*

3
Late Night News

AT 8:25 P.M., TEN DAYS after her first administrators' meeting, Hannah answers her phone at home. In seconds, she learns that Gerald McCloud has been relieved of his duties as superintendent and will no longer be of service to the Summitville School District. When she asks for details from the newly elected board president, Mrs. Wright tells Hannah that she cannot talk in greater detail because of the legalities.

Five minutes later, another phone call comes from Tim Dowling, asking Hannah if she has heard that McCloud had been fired because he totaled the superintendent's school car last night while driving intoxicated.

Hannah asks Tim if the superintendent is all right.

Tim replies, "Oh, McCloud is fine—the car's a gonner, but he's off to find a good lawyer, I'm sure."

As he continues with more of the unfolding saga, Hannah starts to wonder how this will affect her students and staff, as well as her job as principal. After learning additional sordid details, she hangs up, and contemplates on what she needs to do as building leader to prepare her school for the immediate change.

In the best interest of everyone concerned, she decides to personally call her teachers and staff. One by one, she gives each of them the report given to her by the board president. By the time she completes her phone list, she feels saturated with several different versions of what actually happened, based on the town's rumor mill.

Despite the hour of the night, each staff member thanks her for the information and Hannah notices warmth from each of them that she had not experienced before. As she pulls up the white goose down feather comforter from the mahogany footboard and turns off her grandmother's stained glass lamp, she takes time to reflect. She turns the light back on, walks over to her library, pulls out her notebook, and writes her next insight: *Take the time to make the personal call.*

4
Bright Sunny Morning

A WEEK LATER, HANNAH, ALREADY busy at her desk at 6:45 a.m., is cleaning up some paperwork.

"Is that fresh coffee I smell?" asks a kind, resounding voice outside her door.

She looks up and sees a slender, elderly gentleman in a tweed jacket and bow tie, peering over his bifocals.

"Hi, there. Another early bird, I see. I'm Lester Martin Mathews, but my friends call me Maddy, which I hope you will, too," he smiles.

Hannah finds a clean cup and fills it with the hot liquid.

"Do you take cream or sugar?" Hannah asks in a convivial manner, knowing that she is pouring coffee for her new boss, the interim superintendent, who has a stellar reputation in the region.

"Just black; that's all my wife will let me have these days."

Hannah puts the coffee in his left hand and shakes his right. "Dr. Mathews, I mean, Maddy, it is a pleasure to meet you. What brings you out so early?"

"I heard that our new middle school principal is having a student assembly today and wondered if I could possibly be invited."

Hannah is surprised at this gesture. Up until now, no administrator had been in her building, much less asked to attend her functions. "That would be great. Would you like to speak to our students at the beginning of the assembly?"

He acknowledges her invitation. "That would be fine. Just to say hello to them and wish them well in their studies is all I need to do. Other than that, I thought it would be special just to sit in the back and catch up on my 'middle school days.' What is the topic of your assembly today?"

"Character Education. I'm sure you probably heard that we have a few characters in this building," she jokes, anticipating an amusing response.

As he straightens his bow tie, he smiles, "Good character is caught, not taught. Thanks for the coffee. I look forward to meeting your students."

As he turns to leave, he looks around at the ambiance. "My wife would give you kudos on creating a warm and welcoming office."

"Thank you," she beams. Hannah takes his cup, and, as she watches him stately walk out the door, she realizes she has learned another lesson: *Leadership is not whom you play; it is who you are at all times.*

5
Catching Courage

"THANKS, HANNAH, FOR MEETING WITH me on a Friday afternoon. I am sure your desk is full and I appreciate the time you are giving me," shares Maddy, as he motions for her to sit in the upright leather chair across from him. "I thought we would take this moment to get to know each other. During the past week, I had the wonderful opportunity to observe you and your talents. How did you come up with *Leading with Heart* for the theme of your school year?"

"Actually, I reflected on what you said on the first day I met you," she exclaims, as she gazes at his puzzled look. "If you remember, I gave a flippant answer on Character Education. You then took the less traveled path and gave me thoughts to ponder with your response, 'Character Education is caught, not taught.'"

Maddy's eyes glisten with added interest.

She takes time to articulate her thoughts. "This encouraged me to think more in-depth about the needs of children and the urgency that we face in education. As you know, children today are faced with the challenges of becoming productive global citizens, having the Internet become their extended family through the continual use of social networks, without an understanding of how it is conditioning their thought processes. Their perspectives have a shallowness that limits their reaching a higher sense of purpose."

Hannah stops for a second, looking up at Maddy. "Oh, I must be rambling. I'm sorry."

"No, you are not," says Maddy, with a genuine gaze, appreciating her professionalism as he motions for her to continue.

"Well, okay," agrees Hannah. She continues, "They experience virtual reality, which limits their ability to grasp the range of feelings associated with growth and development. They lose the joy and blessings that one can receive when we give to one another—and what it feels like to experience a noble act."

"I like your train of thought. Keep going," he says, encouragingly.

"I started probing for a higher understanding of *why* focus on Character Education—I believe our job as educators is not only to give them the 3Rs, but, also to groom them to lead families, schools, companies, and governments. Therefore, it made sense to me to define *how* we want them to lead—which is how I came up with *Leading with Heart*."

Maddy sits straighter in his chair, conscious of the fact that he is in the presence of an exceptional person. Amazed at the level of awareness in Hannah's gracious tone and spoken word, he clears his throat and says, "Were you always a grown-up?"

With this, she laughs. "I spent that whole evening thinking how I could bring out the leadership qualities in every kid—and, with time and trust, in every staff member. I want to challenge our students to take ownership of their lives and make the most of their talents and abilities. I don't have the answers on how to do it yet, nor have I built the climate to support my vision, but, I do have the dream."

"Ah, and from every great dream comes reality," he says to her. *And, how is she going to do that*, he ponders. His mind wanders back to his first executive session with the board and the comment that Coach

Riley would replace Hannah once he completes his school leadership certification.

"Maddy, can I ask you a question. How did you make change when you were starting out?"

Maddy is a bit amazed at having this question asked of him. Realizing that she expects a more in-depth answer, he responds, "I listened to my inner voice, which is the glue that keeps everything together for the leader who has courage. What is the inner voice? When you close your eyes, listen only to the silence within yourself, and breathe within that silence. It is in that moment when your best decisions are made and the steps to change begin to unfold."

Listening to Hannah's enthusiasm and watching her shine, Maddy feels a renewed sense of commitment to this job, realizing that his interim position could make a positive difference on this school district and his new charge. In an instant he flashes to the memory of his first mentor who cared enough to take the time to show him where the landmines were. A smile comes over his face as he listens to her questions.

After nearly three-quarters of an hour of dialogue, hearing his stories, and brainstorming ideas, their meeting comes to an end. On her way out, Hannah says, "Dr. Mathews, I really appreciate your help."

"Great. I enjoyed working with your freshness of thought and your love for your school. A courageous leader always dares to be bold— to take a chance. Stay focused in the moment and do not let past accomplishments or disappointments influence your decisions. Let's make this a weekly meeting. See you next Friday at 1:00; how's that sound?"

"Perfect," says Hannah. Moving to the door of his office, she turns back and adds, "Thanks for helping me better understand that listening to and acting on your inner voice takes courage."

After she leaves, Maddy thinks out loud. "Let's see, looks like Hannah could benefit from the *3 Cs,* the foundation of the *Chart of*

Change." How his ability to focus on these concepts saved him from many a fall!

Maddy reflects upon his first year as an administrator when his focus was more on following procedure, rather than addressing human needs. He thought he was doing a great job because his mentor was happy with him: reports were done on time; data were collected and analyzed; and the Student Code of Conduct was adhered to, to a "t." The leftover residual of the quality systems that the former principal had implemented made it easy to continue the daily tasks. From management's point of view, it appeared that things were running smoothly.

All was going well, or so it seemed, until the end of the year when the test scores came back. Rather than going up, the scores showed a significant decline. As Maddy honestly reflects, it was not only scores that declined. Faculty motivation was nil. School spirit seemed to have left with the former principal. People were going through the motions of teaching, but their hearts were not in it. There was no unity among staff; school was not a happy place.

Maddy failed to realize that a key aspect of his work was to cultivate a new vision based on developing the strengths of each team member. When he talked it over with a successful principal from another district, who later became the superintendent of Maddy's district, Maddy was introduced to new thinking. This thinking embraced an understanding of a never-ending awareness of service without a hook— meaning without any attachment to the outcome.

After that meeting, Maddy spent a great deal of time reading, listening, and reflecting to learn as much as he could about leading with heart. Over the years, he learned to share his challenges with his wife, Lilly, a highly cited anthropologist. Together, they created the *Chart of Change*, a way of leading an organization to optimize the health, happiness, and productivity of its people.

Perhaps, with time, he could guide Hannah using the same principles that commanded his actions so that she could reach her full potential as a leader. With that, he writes: *#1. CARING: The First Step in Transforming an Organization* in big print and begins to outline his thoughts for next Friday's meeting.

6
Home Is Where the Heart Is

LATER THAT EVENING, MADDY WALKS in, humming a tune, as he sets his hat on the hand-carved settee. He heads toward their newly updated kitchen and calls, "Lilly, I'm home."

With dirt on her hands, carrying a garden spade, Lilly stands by the back door in garden boots and yells, "I'm out here in the backyard." She sets the spade down, pulls off her gloves, and wipes the wisps of graying hair from her eyes.

Stepping quickly toward the backdoor, Maddy embraces her slender frame and gives her a kiss on her warm forehead.

She pulls away from him, saying, "I'm so dirty. Let me clean up first."

"Ah, you are the most beautiful woman on earth," he grins, hugging her close, as he stares into her dazzling blue eyes. Looking at her latest labor of love, Maddy exclaims, "Wow! The colors of these mums are so vibrant!"

"Yes, I'm delighted with this year's selection at the nursery. They're double bloomed," she joyfully utters, as she pulls off the boots and heads to the sink. "How was your day?"

"The day exceeded my expectations. I feel most fortunate—you were right. Being in this interim position has made me see things differently. I can step back and appreciate the journey of what it takes to be a quality leader. You know, I see in this new middle school principal so much of what I was. I also see the vulnerability of the political role that she is in, coupled with her innocent approach. She is trying to do her best and has such a good heart. She truly cares about her school, her staff, and her students."

Lilly hands Maddy an iced tea. He holds the glass with two hands and sips it slowly.

"Thank you, dear. Lilly, you should have seen Hannah with her students—she is so focused on her vision," he smiles. "You would have loved her exuberance!"

He finishes his drink and sets it down. "She wants to make change in this nearly moribund environment. She's the only breath of fresh air they seem to have. That former superintendent must have really done a job on suppressing creativity. And, the sad part is, it sounds like some board members have plans to push Hannah out by the end of the year, to maintain the status quo."

"Well, you've only got a short time to make a difference. So, if you are going to mentor her, you'd better get a move-on. By the way, I picked up the brochures on the new Winnebago. When do you think they will hire the new superintendent?"

"They should have one in a couple of months. They've just started the preliminary profile on what the community needs in an educational leader. Hey, guess who called me today—Sally Weatherford, the superintendent who took my place. She wanted to know what this *ELS* acronym is that all her administrators were referring to—you know, the *Expanded Leadership Spiral?* Seems like they are all saying the phrase, *Love Supreme* and then—they giggle!"

He takes off his jacket and turns to his chuckling wife. "I can't believe that my words are lasting beyond my stay. I've got to find time to coach these Summitville administrators."

Lilly gives him a loving glance, as she pulls her apron over her coveralls to prepare the evening's meal. "So, what is your next move?"

"I think I will share some key concepts and have an administrators' retreat next month, which is not typical of interims, as you know, so I'm sure I'll catch some flack."

"Bravo, my wonderful husband. You are already breathing new life into this district. Just remember the law of non-interference."

"I know," he quips. "Don't obstruct the activity or actualization of another when pursuing your own goal."

"Good. Now, go change for dinner."

7
Board Meeting in the Parking Lot

As FRANK AMBER SWEEPS THE leaves away from the front steps for the board meeting, he sees Coach Riley finally shutting off the lights to the gym and heading toward the parking lot. *Looks like the coach is hanging around to hobnob with the board members again. Wonder how the new supe is going to handle the shenanigans of this board?* contemplates Frank.

Frank whistles his favorite tune, "When Irish Eyes Are Smiling," as he thinks about the bow-tied newcomer. He reflects on the talk that he had with Dr. Mathews a few days earlier. Mathews said that when he came to meet the board for the first time, he noticed that the place was less than sparkling. He told Frank that he believed that cleanliness was next to Godliness and that it was up to the district to be the role model for the students and the community. Frank was relieved to find that someone actually cared about his job.

Now, holding Maddy's email in his hands, Frank goes over his new *to do* list to make sure he's ready for the evening's event:

- Make sure that tables and chairs are all wiped down after the juniors finish using the room for homecoming decorating;
- Make sure that the indoor trash containers are emptied just before the meeting;
- Get maintenance to replace the blown-out bulbs and make sure

all the outside lights and inside lights are on, to accommodate the senior community who may come to the public meeting;

- Make sure that filtered water is used to make the coffee and that the creamers are put on ice because of a concern with the lackadaisical habit of leaving them out to spoil;
- Make sure that the outside flag is lowered at dusk and that there is a permanent flag in the boardroom;
- Have a pad of paper and pencil at every board member's seat;
- Make sure all the leaves are swept away from the front steps and walkways that lead to the parking lot.

Frank gathers a bunch of leaves and bags them to complete his list. From the corner of his eye, he observes the actions in the parking lot. The custodian sees Coach Riley walk over towards his Jeep, carrying the familiar green *First Bank of Summitville* zippered bag.

At the same time, Dan Sterling, a board member who is a director of finance for a Fortune 500 company, pulls up in his BMW convertible.

Coach Riley walks over to Dan's car to greet him.

Dan, dressed in a black three-piece suit, gets out of the car, and gives the Coach a jab in his shoulder. "Hey, Buddy. Still taking those courses? How're they going?"

"Yep, I'm plugging away. I'm taking two this fall and the last two next spring."

"So, you're still on track. Good."

"Our trip to Myrtle Beach isn't going to be the same without McCloud. I was looking forward to taking all his money in the poker games again—and all of Sam's too," jokes Tom, as they both rib each other and laugh.

As they're talking, another board member drives up in a lettered truck: *Venza's Sprinkler Fittings: Safe and Sound.* "Hey, shall we include Pete on our golf trip? He's single and probably can get away."

Dan replies quickly, "No, my wife doesn't get along with him that well, ever since he broke up with her sister's daughter."

"Dan, before Pete comes over, I want to make sure of something. You told that interim that I'm to be the principal once I get my cert., right?"

"Yeah, I mentioned it in executive session. You're fine," confirms Dan, nonchalantly.

Frank overhears them talking about their clandestine outings and shrugs his shoulders as he pushes more leaves into bags. *Sad to know that our elected leaders don't appreciate their ethical responsibilities,* he thinks with a sigh. Frank ties a bag of leaves and carries a couple of the bags to his truck on the other side of the coach's Jeep.

Dan looks over at the custodian. "Hey, should we keep our voices down?"

"Nah," replies Tom. "Frank's harmless."

Ignoring the thoughtless comment, Frank turns his face into the evening shadows, and continues to throw bags onto the truck.

Looking over Dan's shoulder, Tom sees Pete Venza walking toward them, still in his grey work clothes, and waves to him.

Dan turns around and reaches out to shake Pete's hand. "How does it feel to be the newest board member? Do you feel powerful?" he laughs.

They look over to see Sam Golding, the owner of the largest real estate firm in town, lock his Mercedes and grab his unopened packet from the back seat.

Pete changes his board packet into his left hand and shakes Dan's hand. "It feels great. But I don't understand anything in this packet."

Dan gives a smirk as he automatically takes a handkerchief from his pocket to wipe his hand. "All you have to remember is just do whatever

I tell you and vote however I vote. We stand together—so don't worry; we've got your back. We'll cover for you," he says reassuringly, while glancing toward Tom.

Overhearing the conversation, Sam joins in. "Yes, we've got you covered, Pete. I see everyone got here early. Things were comfortable when Jerry was here. Hope this new interim doesn't try to make any changes."

Dan's voice flares with disgust. "Those do-gooder board members moved too fast on this one. McCloud was just coming home from the fundraiser, doing his job."

Sam retorts, "We lost the fight on this one. It's going to be hard to find someone whom we can manage as well," as he winks at Tom.

Tom interjects. "Yeah, we sure miss him here at school—the bow-tie guy isn't nearly as much fun."

The group chuckles.

"Let me get to the bank before it closes. Enjoy your meeting, guys. I'll give you a call later, Dan." As he slides into his Jeep, he turns the key in the ignition, and shuts the door. "Looks like I played this one right," he says out loud, in earshot of the custodian. He waves to the guys and drives away.

Frank Amber pulls the leaf guard over the cab of his truck. His thoughts reflect on the group's chatter: *Guess the coach is still pushing to be the middle school principal.*

When the other board members arrive, the three board members quickly change the topic to talking about the weather as they walk toward the side entrance. They say their simple pleasantries as they greet Mrs. Regina Wright, the board president; Dr. V.J. Sanjay, a family practitioner and Vice President; and two other members: Mrs. Elizabeth Simpson, who runs the board subcommittee for *Parents in Education* forum; and Mr. Benjamin Winters, a former retired teacher.

The tension builds quickly among the board members when Sam

and Dan start hounding Mrs. Wright, questioning her leadership on how she could fire McCloud for such a minor offense. Tempers flair as the members start talking at once.

Mrs. Wright, who had stayed silent throughout the fiery exchange, finally raises her hand to quiet the group. "Look, it was the right thing to do—it was the right thing for the kids, the right thing for the community, and the right thing for us as a board. I know it hurts—I know you enjoyed him as a person, but we cannot condone his egregious breach of conduct. We are role models for this community. Let's get beyond our differences and move forward. We have a lot to do."

Standing at the side entrance of the building, Frank holds the door for the board members to enter. He closes the door after them and sees the lights go out in the interim superintendent's office. Comically, he thinks: *So, I cleaned up the outside of the school, just like you wanted, Dr. Mathews. Now, how are you going to clean up the insiders of the school?*

8
Facilitating Focus

"YOU'RE GOING TO BE LATE for your meeting—it's 3:29 p.m. You know I can't stay late," whines Darci, as she glances at the oversized steel clock hanging on the cement wall.

Hannah picks up her pad and quickly marches to the Conference Room where the Character Ed meeting is to take place. Sitting at the table are selected representatives of the Middle School faculty: Mrs. Jane Lauder, a math teacher, who's considered an old timer and treasurer of the union; Mr. Russell Newhart, one of the first year science teachers who also teaches one period of technology; Mrs. Margarita Alexander, the social studies teacher who is known in the community for co-authoring the Historical Society Yearbook; Ms. Mary Jo Joyner, a music teacher who always has a smile on her face; and Mr. Denzel

Williams, the 8th grade English teacher, who is correcting his students' essays as Hannah takes her place.

"I thank you for giving up your free time to trail blaze a new path for our school," Hannah says, as she smiles a glance towards Mr. Williams, who puts his students' papers away. "I want to thank you for working with community representatives over the last two weeks to better define our theme, Leading with Heart."

"The outcome of those meetings led us to one of this year's goals: to create a stronger bond between our students and our community. Ideally, our community wants our students to raise their families in Summitville and be its future leaders," Hannah continues. "In order for us to reach such a lofty goal, let's state some of the key concepts from last week that we would like to include in our Character Ed program."

Hannah starts writing the concepts on the Smartboard, while Mr. Williams reads them out loud.

"1) An appreciation for those who have guided and protected them along their path of life.

2) A genuine sense of purpose of knowing who they are, and what they can become, aware of the freedoms and choices that they have.

3) A willingness and dedication to give of their time and talents for the good of society."

"Thanks, Mr. Williams, for summarizing our work to date. Are there any other thoughts that come to mind?"

"How about that we add a fourth one: An ability to model honesty and integrity," adds Mrs. Lauder. "That's what I find missing in many of my students. And that could drive our theme."

"Well-stated," compliments Hannah.

Mrs. Alexander chimes in. "It reminds me of how we were taught: My name is only as good as my word."

"Terrific." Hannah continues, "So, now we need some activities to make this fun for all. During my short time in the community, I have met great role models for our students: genuine, caring individuals who have made significant contributions to our school. Talking with these people, I sense a willingness from them to be involved with the growth of our young students. So, let's brainstorm some things we could do that would draw upon the talents and attributes of our community members."

Ms. Joyner, who has jotted a few notes, quickly speaks up. "It has been my experience that if you build it—in this case, the program— they will come. Whenever our kids perform, we fill the auditorium. Grandparents, aunts, uncles, and even alumni come out to see the jubilant faces of our kids, particularly in the elementary school. What if we think about hosting events that would connect our community to our goals?"

"I'm really not sure why we are trying to bring in the community. Isn't that the PTA's job?" questions Mrs. Lauder.

Ignoring her comment, Mr. Williams leans back on his elbow and says, "To get us started, I remember several years ago we had an event where we invited all the senior citizens to visit our school for a day, so they could experience our new technology. Perhaps we could do something like that."

Mr. Newhart enthusiastically jumps in. "In my high school, we always had a Senior Citizens' Day where the seniors came in to give a talk about how schools were valued in their day. Perhaps we could do something like that."

Agreeing, Mr. Williams shares, "I can name a number of senior citizens who are caring and would love to share their thoughts with our students. This is a wonderful opportunity for generations to give to one another."

"Hmmm…, what if we had senior citizens come in and make a website on the Internet, followed by an open discussion on Character

Education with our students," rethinks Mrs. Lauder. "We could actually connect the experiences of the seniors with our students and then have our students help launch the highlights of the day onto the web so that the whole community can benefit."

"Perhaps we can call it 'Gems of Summitville Generations,'" interjects Mr. Newhart.

Ms. Joyner says excitedly. "I've got it—I will have the chorus and band perform a few songs from the 50s/60s."

"Great, what else?" asks Hannah.

"I'd be willing to stay after school with students to write personal invitations to each senior citizen of the community. It would fit right into the Communities and Societies curriculum," beams Mrs. Alexander.

"Our department could have our students write up interviewing questions for the seniors during English classes," smiles Mr. Williams.

"Excellent. These are some terrific ideas and very doable," confirms Hannah.

"We can also hold an 8th grade advisory meeting and help the students understand the importance of the day and how they can best serve this special event," says Mrs. Lauder.

Hannah smiles. "Great work, everyone. Sounds like we're ready to map out the day."

The committee comes to an agreement on the following schedule for the day:

GEMS OF SUMMITVILLE GENERATIONS

1:00-1:30 Registration and Middle School Jazz Band and Chorus perform a few 50s/60s songs
1:30-3:00 Seniors go to technology classes to learn the latest on web design
3:15-4:00 High Tea with seniors and students

4:00-5:00 Students interview seniors on life stories connected
to Character Ed
5:30-7:00 Senior Citizens Dinner—8th grade servers with PTA
help

"Sounds like we have the framework for a terrific day," says Hannah. "And next week I will begin meeting with all students. This will help me learn their interests, and how we, as a team, can better serve them. I will have Darci write up the notes of our meeting tomorrow, summarizing the quality work that you did today. I look forward to seeing you next Thursday to fine-tune our plans to share with the faculty."

When she gets back to her office, she sees a note on her desk from Darci: "Don't count on me tomorrow—I'm having a spa day." Hannah thinks: *Two steps forward, one step back.*

9
Caring: The Cornerstone

THE NEXT DAY WHILE SHE was on her way to the superintendent's office, Hannah finds herself thinking about the Character Ed meeting. It was invigorating to see that Mrs. Lauder started to voice her thoughts on planning the activities, once it was obvious that her role as 8th Grade Advisor was significant to the success of the program. Hannah begins to feel that subtle changes are starting to occur and that the building team is developing a clearer vision. She stops for a minute before walking into his office and writes in her notebook: *When an opportunity presents itself without attachment or fear of rejection, then people can respond objectively, presenting their true thoughts.*

"Ah, I see you are in deep reflection. Anything to share?" asks Maddy, motioning to the open chair across from his desk.

Hannah takes a seat, sets her pad down on her lap, and relays her insights about the prior day's meeting. Maddy, appreciative of the depth of her thoughts, reaches into his top desk drawer and pulls out an index card that says: *#1: CARING: The First Step in Transforming an Organization.* He hands it to her.

Seeing her give a questioning look, he takes her cue.

"I see you are puzzled. Caring is much more than six letters. You just expressed your ability to listen with the desire to understand. That is the way to connect with anyone's heart. It's the first step in transforming an organization to help people reach their leadership potential, to become the best that they can be. By showing that you care about them, they, in turn, share, and what they share becomes their gifts to you," replies Maddy.

"Gifts to me?" asks Hannah.

"Yes, gifts for the leader. And, you need to receive their gifts with gratitude."

Maddy continues. "Caring helps to create a positive setting whereby the exchange of dialogue deposits 'money' in people's self-esteem banks. In this exchange, individuals need to freely communicate with one another. If one person is not allowed to complete his contribution to the dialogue, that interruption can create a withdrawal from his bank."

Listening intently, Hannah asks, "Oh, you mean like the leadership style of McCloud?"

Maddy nods. "Therefore, caring not only gives clarity to purpose, it also creates a balanced exchange without expectation, resulting in an opportunity for individuals to grow."

They exchange ideas and strategies that Hannah can use with her faculty. Hannah realizes that *caring* actually is more than a stepping-stone—rather, *caring* is the cornerstone in building a foundation for leading her school.

"It sounds like you were given several gifts at your meetings. When we meet at our retreat, we will continue to expand on this concept and learn more about a system that really helped me stay focused in the present when I was starting out."

After Hannah closes the door to Maddy's office, she pulls out her notebook and writes: *A caring leader always dares to be candid.*

10
Imagination Meets Passion

By THE THIRD WEEK OF September, Hannah notices that the teachers are getting into a routine as she does her morning walk-throughs. She beams as the sounds of joy coming from Ms. Joyner's middle school chorus rehearsals. She thrills to the interactive discussions in Mr. Williams' writing class. She grins, hearing the theoretical questions asked in Mrs. Lauder's pre-algebra class. But, her walk slows when she observes the dullness in Mr. Conway's study skills class. Each day it seems like the lessons are routine and painful to his students. Their attention is everywhere else but on his words. The only movements of the students that she observes are when they take out their study skills workbooks from their backpacks. As if being tortured, they open their workbook and start on the next assigned page. That concludes Mr. Conway's teaching, as he sits behind his desk and opens the morning newspaper.

The first time Hannah saw Mr. Charles Conway, he was sitting by himself in the back of the library at the faculty orientation meeting. His image is still fresh in her mind. He was wearing a light blue oxford shirt, adorned with a plastic pen protector in the shirt pocket, filled with stainless steel writing tools. When she first observed him teaching the study skills class, he was reading a newspaper. Hannah asked him how the newspaper fit into his lesson. Mr. Conway responded that he was preparing for the next day's lesson on current events. That was over a week ago. As she observes the lack of interaction with his students, Hannah gets that queasy feeling in her stomach. She knows she has to confront this scenario.

Back in her office, she has Darci make an appointment with Mr. Conway for the next morning during his free period and asks Darci for his personnel file.

Darci sets Mr. Conway's file on her boss's desk, with a comment, "Don't expect miracles," as she closes Hannah's door.

Reading the file, Hannah discovers that in his 23 years of teaching, Mr. Conway has had less than stellar observations. It seems that when he first started teaching, he was very imaginative in his thinking and innovative in his approach. He organized student trips to the planetarium with midnight telescope observations. He ran summer enrichment programs where teenagers excavated local caves and developed scaled models of geological time.

His early evaluations accentuated the enthusiasm of his students. But then Hannah finds a disciplinary letter that appeared to mark the beginning of the deterioration in his teaching. It spoke about a lesson on Mohs' hardness scale where Mr. Conway engaged students in an activity that was not within the conventional mode of discovery. In an earth science lab, students were asked to scrape different stones to analyze the hardness of matter.

In one of his lessons, he was trying to prove the hardness of enamel, so he told students to wipe several objects with an alcohol swab and bite gently down on talc and graphite to better understand their density— and laughed when the kids said, "eeooooowww—germs." He reassured them that it was hygienic. Since one student just came back from Ireland, he said that it was definitely more hygienic than kissing the Blarney Stone. With that, the student bit down defiantly on a granite sample and chipped his tooth. It turned out, as Hannah peruses the file, that the parents sued the school and Mr. Conway personally.

Hannah leans back in her chair to understand the impact of such a shattering event on one's teaching. Despite the fact that negligence was not established, Hannah notes that observations after this date were barely adequate. It seems to Hannah that the debacle depleted Mr. Conway's energies. His sparkling, innovative ways dwindled to lackluster teaching. She turns another page and finds a comment on a post-it that says, "Conway no longer effective in motivating students— Move to SS."

Hannah summarizes that his reassignment was to minimize his negative effect on students. She pulls out her notebook and begins to prepare for the next day's meeting by scripting a few probing questions.

At 10:00 a.m. the next morning, Mr. Conway comes to Hannah's door. She shakes his hand and thanks him for coming to her office.

Sheepishly, he takes a seat and peers over his lap to stare at his brown shoes.

"Do you know why I have asked to meet with you today?" she asks the battered employee, in a soothing tone.

Mr. Conway continues to look at the floor and shakes his head.

Hannah tries a more direct approach. "Mr. Conway, what do you like most about teaching?"

Seemingly taken back by the question, he looks up at her with an inquisitive stare.

Hannah gives him a sincere gaze to prompt an honest answer.

Mr. Conway stutters at first, obviously trying to formulate his thinking on a question he has not been asked in a long time. "Ah, I . . . I . . . I . . . I'm not really sure what you're asking," he responds.

Not giving him a reply, so as not to direct his answer, Hannah remains silent. With an intense, but kind look on her face, she uses the silence to encourage him to speak.

She watches him struggle, as his eyes go back to looking at his shoes. A full minute passes with nothing said.

Finally, Mr. Conway breaks the silence, looks up, and smiles, "I see you're not going to let me off the hook on this one."

"You are correct, Mr. Conway. I am very interested in your answer."

Mr. Conway takes a deep breath, seemingly overcoming many emotions. Raising his eyes and looking directly at her, he responds, "I like the 'ah-ha' moment, when kids discover the mysteries of Planet Earth."

"And when did you last experience that?" Hannah prods.

He answers guardedly, "Long before you ever got here. Why do you want to know?"

"Give me a specific moment in your past when you felt such a joy," she pushes.

He looks at Hannah with a new stare. "You're serious. Okay, I had an earth science class a number of years ago, where I had a kid who questioned the big bang theory, only to move into his own discovery of the expanding universe. He became so turned on to scientific discovery that he went on to graduate from MIT, got his Ph.D., and became a nuclear physicist for DARPA."

"That's an incredible story. You must be so proud of your student," Hannah acknowledges.

"Yes, I am," he replies, with renewed strength in his voice.

"To be candid with you, Mr. Conway, I read your file. I know that your skills are not utilized in the position that you are in. If you are willing, I would like to propose a plan to get you back into the science classroom—as a teacher mentor during 3rd period."

She sees him light up. "I was thinking that you would make an excellent mentor for our newest earth science teacher, Russ Newhart. It's not getting you into your own classroom yet, but at least it is a step in the right direction. Would you be interested?"

"Is this an addition to my assignment? How would this happen?"

"We have discretionary money for mentoring. You would get paid a stipend."

"What would I be expected to do?"

Hannah goes over a short list of ideas that he could consider. He looks at her in astonishment, and, realizing that she giving him an opportunity to move out of the shadows of his past, his eyes well up.

Hannah continues. "I know that you have an amazing imagination. If you are interested, go home this weekend, and draw up a plan. Be creative. This *is* your forte," she smiles.

Standing up, she extends her hand.

As he shakes it, he says, humbly, "Thank you for this meeting; this means more than you realize. I'll have an outline on your desk first thing Monday."

"I look forward to seeing it," she smiles, as the passing bell rings loudly. Watching him walk down the hall with a new gait, she thinks to herself: *Listening to your inner voice benefits all.*

11
Goal-Setting Works for Students Too!

HANNAH LOOKS AT HER SCHEDULE that she developed to connect her to every student in her school and walks into the first period 8th grade Math B classroom.

"Good morning, students. I want to thank your teacher, Mrs. Lauder, for allowing me to take this time from her important subject to get to know each of you better. My job as your principal is to 1) keep you safe, 2) allow you to maximize your academic potential, and 3) be available to you as a mentor and as the leader of the team of the people who support your growth to become a future leader."

She hands out 5x7 index cards and has the students put their name on it, their address, their phone numbers, family information, and their birthday. After they completed that much, Hannah says, "I have a toolkit on my desk, but right now it is empty. The tools I need are answers to three questions to help me help you on your journey to develop skills and strong character. Please start writing your responses."

Noticing the famous Euclid print hanging on the canary-colored classroom wall, Hannah smiles and begins her questions as she walks around the room. "Number 1: Write down an academic goal—something that you would like to try for—maybe something you weren't able to do before that will make you feel that you have achieved something great this year. It may be stating that you will complete all your homework each night. It may be stating that you will work to get an A in this class or in a class that you find to be challenging. It may be trying to get on the Principal's List or Honor Roll. It could be preparing for the National Spelling or Geography Bee. Choose anything that will give you a good feeling about your job as a student who is learning."

"Number 2: For the second goal," she continues, "write down something you would like to try for that is extracurricular; something that will connect your interests to your talents. It could be something with art, such as submitting an entry to the Mid-Region Art Festival. It could be with music, perhaps learning another instrument or trying out for the musical, or it could be with sports—trying out for the baseball team or running a community 5K race. It could be running for Student Council or joining the debate team—or any club, for that matter. What is important is your commitment to strengthening your talents and broadening your interests as you learn to work with others."

"Number 3: The third goal helps build character," she states, as she walks behind the desk of a student still writing. "This goal should be one that connects you to others through your kindness. It is an understanding that you are here to be of service to humanity. And, it is learning to accept graciously the gifts given to you. Think of something that you could do for others that also makes you feel good about yourself. It could be raking an elderly person's lawn, volunteering to read books for young children at the library, tutoring someone in a subject that you excel in, or helping our global community in need because of recent earthquakes and floods. The list is endless. How can you be of service? Think of a way that you would like to help others and write it down."

She smiles at the student still writing and moves to the desk of a student on the other side of the room. "And last, think: if you could become anything in the world, what would you like your fulltime career to be? Remember, anything is possible. Write it down."

Hannah encourages dialogue as students share comments with one another. As the students submit their index cards to Hannah, she thanks them and Mrs. Lauder for allowing her to do this important work.

Mrs. Lauder walks Hannah to the door and says, "I have never seen the kids having so much fun connecting their lives with school. Thank you. I think that this is truly going to be a remarkable year."

Chapter 2: October

12
A Coach of a Different Color

"WELCOME, EVERYONE. TODAY'S ASSEMBLY IS an extension of our Character Education leadership program. As a caring school community, we have been exploring how we can become future leaders. Your teachers and your Student Council have been working together to find ways for you to be successful in pursuing your toolkit goals."

Hannah continues in her auditorium voice. "They have identified Internet safety as an important assembly topic to help protect you against Internet crimes, while allowing you to use it as a tool in your learning. We want to thank our Summitville PTA for sponsoring our program today. First on our program, please give a warm welcome to FBI Special Agent Carl Bennett. His job is to come to schools like ours to make students more aware of cyber crimes and Internet bullying."

Agent Bennett comes forward and begins his extensive talk, explaining the dangers of cyberspace. The students are captivated as they listen to the shock and awe approach of the speaker.

Hannah surveys the refurbished auditorium, appreciating the summer overhaul of the new seat cushions for the audience. She marvels at the attentiveness of both her students and faculty. However, she notices two adults in the back of the auditorium whispering to each other and moving out into the hall. Reacting on her instincts—that something is not quite right—Hannah goes out the side door of the auditorium and walks down the hall, wondering what the problem is. She overhears one person saying, "What a waste of time—and money! These kids should have been in gym class with me!"

"It's a new world, Coach," explains the other.

Coming around the corner, Hannah now recognizes the voices as Mr. Riley and Mr. Conway. She sees the back of the coach and hears his response.

"Well, I've got more important things to do. And so do these kids. How are they going to learn anything if they're out of class for this Character Ed nonsense! We're not their parents. I am sure that the test scores are gonna go down the tubes this year. Boy, does that new principal have a lot to learn! She's not going to last. I'm going to my office to make some phone calls."

"Give her a chance. I'm heading back in," says Mr. Conway, as he sees Hannah moving toward them.

"Everything okay here?" asks Hannah, as she watches Mr. Conway return to the auditorium.

"Yeah, I was just getting a drink," says Coach Riley, as he heads toward the water fountain down the hall.

Frank Amber comes around the other corner, carrying a ladder, and whistling softly.

Realizing the stark contrast of the coach's disgruntled behavior to the custodian's exuberance, Hannah revels in Frank's lilting spirit and thinks: *A caring employee lives the climate and lives the joy.*

13
Wristbands to the Rescue

ZACK ZELMAN, AN 8ᵀᴴ GRADE student at Summitville Middle School, throws his backpack on his bed and fires up his laptop on his desk. His room is filled with books, articles, newspapers, computer equipment, and cords. Surrounded in what would look like chaos to most people, he feels calm in this environment where his creative processes thrive. Pushing aside some papers on his table, he opens up his English file on the cloud, and begins to write in his journal:

> *Another day of being invisible. Science class goes so slowly—Kids still asking questions on acceleration—Newhart gave that formula over a week ago and they still don't get it. Velocity over Time— How hard can that be! I forgot my gym clothes again—Never have seen the Coach get so red! At least he let me work on my iPad while the others got hot and sweaty. Got called Geek only 7 times today. I was the only one who knew what an algorithm was for Lauder's class. My mom got me a great book about Alan Turing's machine—on the third chapter already.*

He finishes his journal and closes his file. He then reaches into his backpack to get the rest of his homework assignments and finds the note from his mom that he forgot to give the attendance officer. *Hmm*, he thinks. *I was wondering where that was.* He pushes it aside and pulls out the flyer that he received from his homeroom teacher: *School Improvement Contest: Find a better way to improve the learning environment. First Prize—the latest Apple iPad with Apps.*

Zack doesn't bother reading anything more. With excitement, he begins a new file, as the flyer slides onto the floor. His fingers fly on the keyboard:

> *Learning Environment: books, paper, desks, teachers, computer, lighting, temperature, time—time! Time: time to hand in, time to correct, time to read and analyze, time to get the class started— Ah, it always takes about five minutes to get the class settled and*

take attendance. What if, if—if the teacher had a better way to take attendance? Yes, a computerized way—to connect everyone to the attendance officer's computer.

Zack sits back in his chair for a moment and thinks out the process:

It could connect the teacher's computer to the Attendance Officer's computer. But, that still takes time away from the class. It could have a student input the attendance – but that stops the learning momentarily for that student. How about if there was a way that each student was responsible to key in his attendance? That would save time for the teacher—but does it cause a line-up at the teacher's computer? Need something—some kind of system that quickly records each kid's attendance.

Needing time to assemble his thoughts, he heads toward the refrigerator and pours a glass of milk. He picks up the remote and clicks on the TV. As he surfs the channels, his hunger stops him at the Oreos commercial. He watches the cashier scan the item and put it in the bag, whereby the buyer pulls out the cookies, rips opens the package, and offers one to the cashier, as the logo banner appears: "Make New Friends."

He searches the cabinets, but no Oreos. Settling on a peanut butter and jelly sandwich, he heads back to his room. Still thinking about those Oreos, it comes to him: *Why can't kids scan their way into a classroom!*

With that, his mind races as he begins his computerized design. He designs a few prototypes, but the challenges of cost and logistics make him start anew. About five hours later, he finally yells, "Eureka—move over, Archimedes, there's a new kid in town!"

14
A Parent's Worst Nightmare

IT IS THE THIRD WEEK of October. As Hannah is driving to her office, she reflects on the quality conversations that she has had with her dedicated educators over the past few weeks. She feels a genuine connection with them as they begin a new approach to implement the foundations of Character Education within each of their subjects.

Pulling into her parking spot at the usual time of 7:00 a.m., Hannah is surprised to find a parent waiting for her outside the building. *Ah, it looks like Jamie Randall's mom*, she thinks to herself, wondering what she wants. She parks her car and walks to the door to let both of them in. As she gets closer, she sees Mrs. Randall's tear-stained face. "Are you all right?" Hannah asks.

"No, not really," Mrs. Randall confides. "Can I meet with you in your office privately?"

"Of course," Hannah replies, compassionately, as she opens the door to let Mrs. Randall in.

When they get into her office, Hannah asks, "Can I get you a cup of coffee or some tea?"

"Actually, tea would be quite nice; thank you."

While the tea is brewing in the automatic machine, Hannah takes Mrs. Randall's coat from her and hangs it up. "Jamie is such a bright girl—I know she has been out a lot lately. Is she okay?"

"That's why I came to see you this morning, Ms. Gardner," she says, as Hannah gives her a cup of tea in a flowered coffee mug, along with some honey and milk. "I don't know how to share this—it's hard to say what I need to say."

Hannah, making a cup for herself, closes the office door, and sits next to Mrs. Randall. "Please, what is troubling you?"

Mrs. Randall proceeds to tell Hannah that Jamie has been feeling very run-down and not able to stay awake for long periods of time. "Jamie's appetite has changed from a starving teenager who was always eating to a girl who just doesn't feel like eating much. In fact, she even fell asleep at the dinner table two weeks ago. She started to develop sudden bruises, sometimes from simple things, like leaning up against her seatbelt in the car. She's always been such an active child—with field hockey and volleyball teams—so when she became lethargic and started sleeping late, I took Jamie to the doctors. They found that Jamie's blood work revealed that she suffers from acute myeloid leukemia, better known as AML. The news was devastating."

"Oh, my goodness," consoles Hannah. "I've never heard of AML. What does that mean?"

"Neither had we. But what I now understand is that AML affects various white blood cells and Jamie will have a long battle ahead. Yesterday, new results came back to confirm what the doctors suspected. Jamie has leukemia."

Startled by this dramatic news, Hannah reaches across to take Mrs. Randall's hand. "Oh, Mrs. Randall. Poor Jamie. What happens next?"

Mrs. Randall breathes a heavy sigh. "Well, it means more tests and most probably, we are going to have to make a decision fairly quickly if we are going to begin treatment for her." With that, her eyes well up.

Hannah gets out of her chair, gives Mrs. Randall a tissue, and puts her arm around her. "Oh, I am so sorry. This must be so hard for you. What can I do for you?"

"I thought we could handle this just within our family. So sorry to have to also involve you," Mrs. Randall says, wiping her eyes as she tries to regain composure. "Thank you for caring."

"We're a team. Never doubt it." Hannah squeezes Mrs. Randall's hand and moves back to her chair.

Mrs. Randall gives an appreciative look to Hannah. "My husband said you would be comforting. He remembers you from the Opening Day. Remember? You had a nice talk with him about his job." She blows into another tissue and puts it into the wastebasket.

"I'm okay now," she replies, as Hannah sees Mrs. Randall take a deep breath, obviously, to calm herself. "The doctors have told us that Jamie is going to miss a considerable amount of school—but she loves it so much. She's so afraid that she will have to repeat 8th grade. Is there anything you can do?"

"First and foremost, it is most important that Jamie gets well. That's really the only priority right now. In terms of schooling, according to our policy for students with a prolonged illness, a student needs to be out for two weeks before homebound instruction begins," relays Hannah in a consoling voice. "In the meantime, we can get homework assignments and the books from her teachers. What else do you need?"

"Is there any chance, Ms. Gardner, if she completes her work satisfactorily, that she can go into high school at the end of the year?"

"Yes, if she is well enough to study and complete her work, she should be able to keep up with her peers," says Hannah, allaying the mother's fears. "What other concerns do you have?"

"Jamie is worried about how her peers are going to take this. I am not sure how we should handle this. Do you think that it is better to let her friends know now or should we wait?"

"I think that under the circumstances, her classmates should know. In small towns, news travels fast. This way her friends can learn about it in a positive, nurturing way. This should help Jamie with her challenge—and also help her friends stay connected. I can share the information with the teachers and help them communicate the correct message. How does that sound, Mrs. Randall?"

"Yes, I think that would be very good. If the teachers and her friends keep connected to her, that will help her emotionally at this time."

"Certainly, we can help in that regard. I'll meet with the teachers to come up with a plan to ensure that Jamie has all the support she needs from our end to succeed."

"Thank you for listening and understanding, Ms. Gardner. You are so special. We are so lucky to have you here."

As Hannah takes the empty cup from Mrs. Randall's hand and helps her with her coat, Hannah smiles and says, "Today is the beginning of Jamie's healing process. We are all here behind her. I know that there will be some rough days ahead and you never have to apologize; my door will always be open to you."

With that, Hannah gives Mrs. Randall one more hug and guides her to the front door.

Hannah turns back to her office. She passes by Darci, who is just taking off her coat.

"Wasn't that Mrs. Randall? How come her daughter's been absent so much? What did they do, go to Disneyland or something?" assumes Darci, prying for more information.

As Hannah closes her door, she hears her secretary mumbling something about inventory of pencils and stationery. Hannah sits in the chair where Mrs. Randall sat and puts her head in her hands. *How could this happen to such a young child!*

She grabs her planner and writes: *Develop key communicator plan for Jamie*. With that she moves to her desk, switches on her computer, and logs onto the Internet. She types: *Children and Leukemia* in the search window and clicks: *Go*. With great concern, Hannah prints out the information, puts it in her planner, and refocuses her attention onto the day's events.

15
Tech for the Times

REFLECTING ON THOUGHTS SHE HAD in her leadership classes that sensitive information such as Jamie's condition should be shared with the superintendent right away, Hannah calls him. "Hello, Maddy? Hannah here. Do you have a moment to talk?"

Hannah tells the story regarding Mrs. Randall and her daughter.

The superintendent responds with, "First of all, thank you for sharing this with me in a timely fashion. This certainly allows everyone to be on the same page, which should help in the healing process. So, may I ask, what are your plans from here?"

Hannah starts to rattle off from her note pad. "First, I need to address the faculty and support staff so as to kindle a kind spirit from each of them. I want to brainstorm with the staff to come up with inspirational ways on how we can make sure that there is a unified message of hope and compassion to be shared appropriately with our students."

"Compassion," Maddy states, "is the opportunity to unify, creating one voice. One more thought to consider." Maddy reminds her, "This may be the first time that any of them have faced such a disturbing circumstance. Also, you may find that some staff may be more upset because of past experiences—and you need to be ready to address such fragile conditions."

"Thank you, Maddy..." A silence comes over the phone.

"I hear your thoughts—what else do you need?"

"Well, I did review the home tutoring policy and was wondering if we could get the board's approval for Skyping as an alternative to home visits."

"That sounds innovative. Is that all?"

Hannah stutters. "I do have one more thought. Do you think that we could add student tutoring support via Skyping as a way of connecting kids to kids?"

Maddy laughs. "I hope you will be with me at the board meeting to help me explain the need for these 'in with the time' changes!"

As Maddy hangs up the receiver, he smiles at Hannah's embracement of the value of change. With that, he pulls the fountain pen from his breast pocket. He makes Hannah's next card and writes: *#2: CHANGED CONSCIOUSNESS: Courage to Accept a Conscious Change* in big print. He outlines some thoughts for next Friday's meeting, acknowledging her fearlessness to welcome change.

Leaning back in his chair, he reflects upon past memories. His mind drifts to the time when, as a principal, one of his young students was diagnosed with cancer. The student's parents did everything they could to get the boy to the best oncology program in the nation and even flew him to Lourdes, France, hoping for a miracle. The small community banded together to deliver healthy meals each night to the family on a rotating basis. Business owners sent anonymous checks to help with the additional financial burdens. Teachers made home visits to tutor the student and took no money from the district. Maddy remembers that he personally went to the home several times. His hardest visits were when he went to the hospital to show his support.

A smile comes over Maddy's face as he remembers during that time when a group of students came to his office one morning and respectfully asked if a policy could be changed. That policy was the "no hat" policy, which Maddy ardently implemented.

When Maddy asked why, the students said, "Because Alan is coming back to school tomorrow for half a day, but he's embarrassed to come because he has no hair."

Maddy still remembers the joy on every student's face, when not only did all the students in Alan's class wear hats the following day, but also Maddy, himself, walked in with a baseball cap on his head!

With pen in hand Maddy continues to write: "When a creative idea comes, the courageous leader taps into the unlimited resource of love. It comes in a heartbeat. All the leader has to do is have the courage to embrace it and act upon it."

Putting the cap back on the pen, his thoughts drift to another time and place on how a change of consciousness helped him and Lilly recover when they lost their only son in combat. With that, he picks up the phone to call her to see if she wants to go out for dinner.

16
A Romantic Evening

THE CRESCENT MOON WAS RISING over the evergreen trees in the distance. A few stars were already twinkling as Maddy opens the door for Lilly to enter their favorite Italian restaurant.

After ordering from the menu, Maddy affectionately takes Lilly's hand and shares thoughts from his day. "My lovely flower, so many times during the day, our spiritual journey together guides my direction to lead with heart."

Squeezing his hand gently, Lilly responds, "This sounds interesting. Do tell what you are thinking."

Maddy turns her hand over and gives it a quick kiss. They release their hands naturally and open their napkins.

"Well, today, Hannah called me with a challenge: one of her students has leukemia and she is anticipating the impact that such a scenario can have on her school, as well as on the child and her family."

"Oh, how sad for the family," Lilly says, consolingly.

"You are so right," agrees Maddy. "Then Hannah started talking about kindling a kind spirit to ensure that her students get a unified message of compassion. She called me to verify a solution. She asked me to change our board policy to include Skyping—video conferencing. Do you believe this kid! That makes me think about the time when the students wanted me to change the *no hat* policy for Alan. Remember, I was very attached to that policy."

Lilly giggles at the memory, as she takes her napkin to cover her smile, recalling how hard it was for her husband to relinquish his authority.

"In my deliberation," he continues, "it was you who asked me, 'What is the *right* policy?' and it was you who reminded me that to come from the higher self is simply to let go."

"Ah, my dear one, you give me too much credit. You know our discussions are always a spiritual experience—and I lose track of who said what. Our journeys are often beyond thinking," she laughs.

Maddy takes a drink of water and looks into her inviting eyes. "And it was you who shared my joy when I walked out of our house the next morning with my baseball cap on," he smiles, admittedly. "So, can I take the liberty and stretch our thoughts?"

As she nods with a knowing glance, he asks, "Is there always another step in the discovery of the abundance of creativity available to the individual?"

Lilly takes a moment to respond. "I believe," she says softly, as she leans toward him, "that the creative self is tied to your higher level of consciousness."

As he moves closer to hear her lowered tone, she continues. "Your ability to problem-solve becomes effortless and succinct. Your skills and knowledge level become more enhanced as the light and brilliance within awaken dormant talents. There's an awareness of synergy—a feeling—like being in a cosmic slipstream with actions that foster the greater good."

She looks lovingly into his blue eyes. "The only step you have to take is to focus your attention."

He continues her thoughts. "Well, then, that means that as one pushes toward a higher consciousness, the person comes to the realization that she is more than just a physical or mental being—that she is a spiritual being, powered by love." He puts his hands around the warm base of the candle on the table. "This is the essence of my next meeting with Hannah on changed consciousness."

Lilly, with penetrating eyes and clear tonality in her voice, expands their conversation. "Ah, my dear husband, you are at the top of your game. How fortunate for Hannah to be mentored by your golden heart! You have the opportunity to be gutsy and pass on our conversations, our stories, and our understandings to the next generations of leaders. What do you have to lose?"

She looks at him with knowing eyes.

"A better question," he smiles, "is what does the world have to gain?"

Just then, a gust of wind shakes the outer pane of the restaurant's large window.

Lilly and Maddy watch the autumn leaves spiral in the air. As their hot soup arrives, they exchange a deep and tender moment.

17
Hannah Takes a Stand

"DARCI, IS THE PROGRAM DONE for tomorrow's open house?" asks Hannah, entering the office with her observation folder in her hand. "I need to see the final copy before you run them off."

"Actually, I was going to finish that this afternoon. I have a few other things to do first," sheepishly responds Darci, without eye contact.

"What are you working on?" questions Hannah.

"Next year's county football schedule."

"For whom? Who told you to do that?" asks Hannah, with a bit of irritation in her voice.

"Coach Riley needs it by this afternoon for his county meeting."

The phone rings and Darci answers a parent call.

Hannah feels a wrenching in her stomach, knowing that this way of thinking from school employees will compromise the district's vision for obtaining excellence. Her inner voice commands her thoughts, making Hannah aware that she needs to confront this behavior head-on, despite the fact that Hannah has addressed other non-acceptable actions of Darci.

When Darci hangs up the phone, Hannah commands, "Darci, I need to see you in my office—now."

Alarmed by the firmness in her boss's voice, Darci turns away, and then slowly turns back. "Okay," she says, quietly.

Closing the door behind Darci, Hannah motions for her to sit down. "Darci, tomorrow is the SMS Open House for this community. We are going to have several hundred parents walk through our doors. They will expect nothing less than excellence from us. We are going to be judged on our presentation and our attention to detail. This includes a well-written program that reflects the quality of education that we are providing their children. The program that you are formatting is critical for good public relations. It needs to have no errors—no omissions—no misspellings of names—and to have clear directions to guide parents throughout their visit. This needs to be your first priority, because I need time to review it—and I want it printed today, because I do not want to leave anything to chance for tomorrow."

Darci's body language reveals that she is shocked by Hannah's directness. Showing a defensive posture, her eyes widen and her back stiffens, as she folds her arms protectively across her chest. Throughout Hannah's rebuke, Darci remains silent.

Hannah continues her directive. "Now, I need you to put the

football schedule—as much as you have completed so far—into the coach's mailbox with a note saying that this is all you could do with such a short notice. Got it?"

A nod indicating compliance comes from Darci.

"Good. When can I expect the final draft?"

"I will have it on your desk in an hour," Darci robotically replies.

"And we will review it together as soon as you have it done. That should give you plenty of time to print it out before you go home today."

Darci stands up. "Fine. Is that all?" Without waiting for a response, she turns and walks directly back to her desk.

Hannah takes a look out the window, and then sits behind her desk. She opens up her top drawer, takes out Maddy's card with *#1: CARING* and grimaces. *Is this what Maddy means by gracious gifts?*

18
Open House Night

AFTER MOST OF THE PARENTS have left the building, Hannah sits at her desk and reflects on the evening's happy event, meeting so many caring parents at her first open house. As she starts writing up her summary report of the evening for the superintendent, Russ Newhart knocks on her door.

"Do you have a moment? I know you're tired, but I just wanted to share something with you."

Seeing her first year teacher in her doorway, she motions for him to step in. "What's up, Russ? Everything okay?"

"Actually, the night went fairly smoothly—much better that I anticipated—and my nerves subsided as the evening went on," he smiles. "Parents were very appreciative and I thought they would never stop talking. However, there was something that came up several times and I just wanted to make you aware of it."

With interest, Hannah puts down her pen and moves her papers aside to give him full attention.

He continues, "Remember my student, Zack Zelman? You know, the one who is really bright and aces all the state exams? The parents call him "The Little Professor" and, even though they don't understand him, the parents still remember when he would come over to their houses when he was in elementary school and show their kids how to override the parental controls so the kids could get onto YouTube to see their favorite groups perform."

Hannah shakes her head and chuckles. "So, why are they telling you this?"

"Well, it seems that his computer wizardry has escalated—and it has the parents concerned. He's now figured out a way to connect his classmates' mobile devices together—and they all can see each other's tweets in real time. The kids think it's cool, but the parents are obviously upset, because they don't know what else could develop from these connections."

"That's interesting. So what are the parents doing?"

"They've left messages with Zack's mother, but no one is responding. They want to know if the school can help."

"And what did you say? What do they think we can do?"

"They're wondering if we know about his talents and if we're monitoring him. I told them that I monitor his school work and that it's their job to oversee their children's activities at home."

"Sounds like you responded appropriately."

He pauses. "Zack is brilliant, but he seems bored in class. I don't know how to challenge him anymore."

Hannah queries, "What kinds of things are you doing in class?"

"Well, we're working on data analysis, but he whizzes right through that. He's always turning on his iPad as soon as he completes the assignments—which is in about half the time of anyone else. And when I ask him what he is working on, he says he's making the school better. He's excited about your contest. He hasn't told me what he is doing—his mom is probably helping him."

Realizing an opportunity, Hannah asks, "Russ, is he a trustworthy kid? I mean, how would you feel about giving him an extra assignment, interfacing with other students where you wouldn't be able to watch him all the time."

"He's a terrific kid. He's very dependable—extremely reliable and usually, he shares his ideas with me—it's just that this time, because it's a contest, he says he wants to surprise me."

"That's cute. Listen, I have a thought. You know that Jamie Randall's mom came in this week to tell us that Jamie needs a tutor while she undergoes her treatments. How do you feel about making Zack as the Science Fair partner for Jamie? They could use Skype as they work on their project together."

"That's a great idea—and I can set it up in class so they can work together during my teaching time to make the science lessons more understandable for Jamie. We can set up the laptop right on Zack's desk—or he can use his own." He pauses and says, "Obviously, that will be on her good days."

"Terrific! I know this means more work on your part. I really appreciate it and I am sure, so will Jamie and her parents. Let's go forward with this thought. We'll talk more in detail tomorrow. Safe ride home."

As Hannah watches him leave the office, she smiles to herself and takes out her notebook to jot down their conversation, then adds: *Once a thought opens to the creative flow, an opportunity will present itself.*

19
Darci's Choice

THE DAY AFTER THE SMS Open House, Hannah greets Darci as she walks in.

Darci takes off her coat and just gives a nod back.

"Darci, before the phones start ringing and the staff come in, I want to finish our conversation from the other day. I just made coffee for us—why don't you get a cup for yourself and come in," says Hannah, in a kind, but authoritative tone.

Darci rolls her eyes and proceeds to fill her cup. She walks into Hannah's office and takes a seat.

As Hannah pulls out a yellow notepad, she says, "First, I want to thank you for doing a great job, making sure that the open house was successful."

"How was the turn-out?" Darci asks in a flat tone, as she holds the warm cup for comfort, obviously hoping to encourage small talk.

Hannah replies, "I was impressed with the attendance—many fathers even came. I think your perpetual flyers encouraged them to come."

Darci does not respond to the compliment.

Sensing Darci's resistance, Hannah puts down her pad and adjusts herself in her chair. "Darci, since I arrived three months ago, I have noticed unacceptable decorum from the person I consider to be my Number 1 *go to* person."

Darci looks uncomfortably at her cup and takes another sip of coffee.

A silence comes between them.

"Darci," Hannah waits for Darci to look up, and then Hannah looks directly into her eyes. "I want to tell you something that's been on my mind and I prefer to be candid."

Although Hannah watches Darci's body become more rigid, this does not deter her from her objective.

"At times," Hannah states, "I feel that we are in an adversarial relationship, rather than acting as partners. I need to trust that you and I are on the same page."

Hannah pauses to watch Darci's response.

Darci gives her a questioning look.

"Let me share with you some of my observations since I've been here." Focusing her delivery so as not to come from an emotional frame of mind, Hannah continues. "At times I have found you critical of parents, critical of students, and critical of teachers. Your side comments often put people down. Giving you the benefit of the doubt, I am not sure if you realize it. It seems to have become a habit for you."

Hannah pauses again, waiting for a reaction from Darci.

Darci shuffles in her chair, turning briefly toward the door, and then turns back.

Hannah continues, strengthening the tone in her voice, but keeping it low. "I need you to remember that we are at the service of this community. As the principal, I am at the helm of running this school for our terrific students. As the secretary, you are more than just support for the clerical functions of this school. You interface with every faculty, every student, every parent, and most community members."

Hannah stops talking and looks at Darci, who has turned her eyes to the window.

Taking a deep breath, Darci turns back with a reddened face and says, defiantly, "Frankly, I have held my job for twenty-eight years. No one before has ever complained about my performance. Principals have come and gone and I am always left to dock the ship."

Darci's eyes begin to tear as she continues her rebuttal. "All I know is that everything is on my shoulders," Darci bursts out as her voice grows louder. "And everybody needs things done right away. I am just doing the best I can!"

Hannah takes a deep breath, allowing the emotions in the room to diminish, as she hands Darci a tissue. "Darci, no one is questioning that you are trying to do your best. There is more to this conversation."

Seeing Darci regaining her composure, Hannah says, "We are the key players in making sure this school runs efficiently and effectively. You are right, so many look to you to aid them in completing their work."

Hannah's tone becomes emphatic as she continues. "And sometimes, because of your strong abilities, they think nothing of asking you to do their job. Before you know it, you are doing double work. They wear you down. This affects you emotionally and drains your energy. It also causes you to lose sight of the big picture, which usually is where my responsibilities lie. And when you place other's work in front of mine, you weaken my effectiveness."

Silence fills the air.

"There's no question, Darci. Your skills are top-notch."

Darci calmly states, "I guess I didn't see it that way. I just thought that you wanted me to do everything. And since you've come on board, everybody's been producing so much more—so there's so much more for me to do then what I did for all the other principals combined."

Hannah and Darci look at each other and burst into a light laughter, enjoying a moment of unanticipated mutual respect.

"Look," says Hannah, "you have to first enjoy your job, which I think you do. But when they start making demands on you, let them know that first you have to get approval from me."

Darci nods in agreement.

"With that understood, there is a second piece. Darci," Hannah adds in a frank tone, "no matter how stressful the job is, first and foremost, your health and well-being are paramount to this position. I promise that I will help you make this job less stressful and more fun. We will set aside a block of time each week to make some action plans, now that the open house is over."

"I would like that very much—just think, a real plan amid chaos," Darci grins.

"One last thing," says Hannah. "I need you to promise me that you have the energy to show compassion—no matter how tired you are—to all who pass your desk, either in person or on the phone. Is that agreeable?"

As Darci smiles in agreement, they both stand and walk toward the door. Darci turns the knob, looks back to Hannah, and says, "No one before has ever taken the time to help me realize the magnitude of my job in a way that I could understand it. I have a new appreciation for my position—thank you."

"You're welcome, Darci."

Hannah watches Darci as she goes to help a teacher who has jammed the copy machine. The words of her mentor, *Caring can inspire a proper perspective and be the bridge to honest communication*, make her smile as she realizes a gift was just given to her.

20
A Change in the Chatter

SITTING AROUND THE LUNCH TABLE in the faculty lounge, Mrs. Lauder takes her salad and a small sandwich from her bag and joins the lunchtime conversations amid her colleagues.

"This year definitely has a different feel. I can't tell if it's the kids that are different—or having a new principal—or the new Character

Ed program, but, believe it or not, I am already up to the unit on Pythagorean theorem. And the kids seem to be really into learning."

"Yeah, you're right. After the first few weeks, I don't think that I have had one behavioral problem. The kids walk in, sit down, and come prepared. It's like they think it's their job."

"Ah, but this is still the honeymoon period. Let's see what the next month brings. You know they usually fall off just before the holidays."

"And then their calendar fills up with parties and school becomes an extension of their social network."

"Well, I certainly like the fact that the kids come in prepared. That, to me, is refreshing. It makes me feel that my job is valued."

"I think the kids feel empowered for the first time. They feel like it's their school and they're happy to be here."

"Yeah, yesterday, Danny Greco, you know the one who was always in trouble last year, actually asked if he could have a tutor to help him prepare for his Algebra test. That's pretty remarkable. And then, Sheila Finestein volunteered to help him. Said she needed it for *Goal 3*."

"The SMS Open House was better attended this year. The parents seemed more aware of what their kids' studies were about and many of them were pleased that they were coming home, talking about school."

"I have found that parent emails have been more focused on how *they* can help rather than how *I* can do my job better."

They all laugh. Just then first year teacher, Molly Dearfield, comes in and they burst into "Happy Birthday."

With an embarrassing smile, she nods her head in acceptance, as pictures are taken.

The candles are lit and Russ Newhart calls out, "Make a wish, Molly!"

21

First Administrators' Retreat: Sustained Energy

"BAGELS, SCRAMBLED EGGS, AND HOT coffee are ready for you," greets Maddy, as each of his administrators enters the door of the Chamber of Commerce Executive Board Room.

The administrative team's voices sound cheerful and somewhat excited to hear what the interim superintendent has to say as they take their places in the lavish surroundings, a stark contrast to their daily work environment.

"Thanks everyone, for being here on this lovely, crisp autumn day. I suppose you are wondering why an interim would want to hold a retreat. You're probably thinking that I won't be here long enough to see anything through."

Soft laughter fills the room.

"There's some truth in that," acknowledges Maddy. "But I wanted to share my thoughts and hear your perspectives during this short time that I am with you."

He looks at the approving smiles around the room. "And, if you don't mind, I would like to stretch your thinking to enhance your ability to lead while reducing the amount of energy that you expend each day. Are you ready?"

Eyebrows raise as looks rivet around the table.

Maddy begins the session by having them solve a problem together with geometric shapes to make a whole puzzle. The group giggles and resembles a kindergarten class more than school leaders, as they playfully engage in the activity.

At the completion of their game, Maddy calls the team back to ask them why they think he started the meeting with a game.

"I guess you want us to remember how we started as students," says Carl Evans of the Garden Elementary School.

Bob Walton from the high school puts down his doughnut and says, "You probably want us to wake up—after all, Saturday is usually my only time to sleep in."

Others laugh in agreement.

With a warm smile, Maddy remarks, "It's those reasons and more. I hope that together this morning we can discover new ways to refresh our commitment to leadership. After all, I know you have demanding jobs with little support and even fewer accolades."

People around the table look seemingly surprised by his comments.

Maddy interprets the look on their faces, wondering if they're thinking that this is going to be a wasted Saturday. He plunges forward with his plan. He hands each of them a tablet of linen bond paper. Next, he opens his briefcase and pulls out beautifully wrapped fountain pens and gives one to each. "I don't know about you, but I find my best thinking comes when I have the best tools. And, don't worry, Tim," adds Maddy as he looks over to the business administrator, "these are gifts from me."

The administrators open their gifts and sparkle when they see the quality of the pens and note the additional refills included.

Maddy continues. "At the beginning of the year, your pen is filled with ink. To maintain the high performance of this pen, you will need to keep the reservoir filled. How can we use this analogy for leading our schools?"

Tim Dowling quips, "Ask for an increase in the budget line?"

The group chuckles.

As more serious answers follow, Maddy realizes that he is ready to move forward to the next stage. "Good, so what I would like to do this morning is to connect you to your personal professional goals, prior to working on our school and district goals. First, I would like to guide you by discussing a concept that I think will help all of you refuel and keep you in peak performance. Sound okay?"

Maddy takes another sip of coffee as he acknowledges the agreements expressed in the room. "Good. At the onset of each school year, we approach our jobs charged and renewed. Throughout the year, our energies are tapped for various reasons because of the demands put upon us. By the time we get to the end of the school year, most of us are running on fumes."

Carl Evans pipes up. "Fumes? By this time I am calling AAA!"

His comment helps transition the group into a less formal atmosphere.

"So, are you ready to move to a higher conceptual level to explore new ways to enhance your leadership staying power?" Seeing everyone perk up, Maddy continues. "Okay—let's get going! I'd like you to use your pens and write down five ways that you, as an individual, replenish your energies. Examples might be that you go to the gym to work out or drive the longer, scenic way home."

Maddy watches them fully engage in the activity. When they finish the exercise, he asks them to tear the paper from the tablet, and on the next page, write five things that they have done or plan to do that energize a community for school renewal. He gives them an example of designing a playground for the school where the whole community takes part in the building of it.

This activity takes a little longer. They seem to have a difficult time getting started. He quietly observes them, careful not to interfere with their thinking. Hannah is the first to actually start writing.

When they complete their lists, Maddy asks them to prioritize the ten responses by stating, "Give a rank of 10 to the thing that gives you the greatest feeling of accomplishment over the long term. Give a rank of 9 to the second most, and so on. You are prioritizing the things that make you most proud."

Then he asks them to rate their prioritized list, giving each a value of 1, 5, or 10, with *1=Good for One*, *5=Good for Some*, and *10=Good for All.*

On the easel, Maddy draws the beginnings of a graph with *x* and *y* axes. He writes *1-10* on the *x* axis and labels it *Sustained Energy.*

He writes *1-10* on the *y* axis and labels it *Leadership Service.*

Maddy asks for their individual responses and plots them on a graph:

Model: SUSTAINED ENERGY

```
L    10  Good for All (Points to View)
e
a     9                                    Help the community build a playground
d
e     8
r
s     7
h
i     6
p
      5  Good for Some        Take the boys fishing
S
e     4
r
v     3
i
c     2        Go to the gym and work out
e
      1  Good for One  (Point of View)
     ------------------------------------------------------------------------------
            1    2    3    4    5    6    7    8    9    10
         S u s t a i n e d   E n e r g y
```

"What do you think this graph means?" prompts Maddy, looking at the puzzled faces.

After a few moments, Hannah finally says, "It looks like the more we interact with an expanded point of view—meaning, for the greater good—the more we are able to renew our energies."

"Wow," says Tim. "How did you get that so fast, Hannah!"

Maddy smiles. "Excellent." With that, he graphically draws the trend line to demonstrate, with clarity, Hannah's insight. "This means that the best way to renew our energies is to work for the greater good, which comes from an expanded viewpoint. And isn't that the heart of leadership?"

Bob sets his pen down and looks perplexed. "It's a nice graph, but what does this mean to me? After all, this is my nineteenth year as high school principal. I'm starting to have students who are the children of my former graduates. I think that eventually everything I do is for the greater good."

Maddy takes a deep breath. "You're right, Bob. In your leadership role, whether you are the principal or the business administrator, initially, you focus on your immediate responsibilities to support effective teaching and to foster a healthy learning environment. Eventually, all that you do impacts the greater good. What this exercise highlights is getting you to consider an expanded point of view with *every* leadership action you do. When we refocus our attention to come from a point of view that embraces the greater good, we allow our higher self—the imaginative faculty—to open to new possibilities, thereby, creating a surge of energy. Decision-making becomes less laborious, minimizing the drain on our energy supply."

Carl jumps in. "Bob, I've been here almost as long as you have. Tell me, when was the last time we ever had a dialogue like this?"

Bob laughs, as Carl turns to Maddy and asks, "Can you give us more insight?"

"Be glad to. Exploring this a bit further, this intrinsic appreciation for a greater consciousness clarifies, ignites, and fuels our efforts." Maddy senses the group's willingness to continue. "Would it be fair to say that a key element of a natural leader is someone who revels in serving the expanded universe?" questions Maddy.

This sparks an active group discussion among the participants as their minds open to new patterns of thought.

Just before lunch, Maddy reminds them that leaders always have another step to take in realizing their potential. He asks them to think about their short and long-term career goals and to come up with three personal professional goals to prepare for the afternoon session.

After lunch, Maddy leads a goal-setting session to develop their school and district goals for the year, while each is cognizant of his/her personal professional goals. Each leader is asked to present one goal while the rest of the leaders show their support by suggesting ways to ensure its success.

Maddy relishes in the thought that his team is humming along. Seeing that the time has flown by, he knows that he needs to bring closure to their day. "I would just like to say, for the short time we have been together, I am happy to be your colleague and appreciative of your dedication to our district. I would like to leave you with one last thought to think about on your drive home."

Maddy stands up to give his final thought. "You can call yourself successful when your staff realizes that the reason you are here is to give service. You can call yourself a master when your staff realizes that it is also the reason they are here. We'll take another step when we meet again," concludes Maddy.

Looking forward to their next meeting with this unique mentor, the administrators gather their new possessions.

Maddy shakes each one of their hands and wishes them a good evening.

They open the door to see the afternoon sun glistening over Summitville.

Chapter 3: November

22
Two to Tango

WITH THE SUN SHINING ON the ice-covered windowpane, Hannah gleefully changes her heels at the end of her day and puts on her sneakers. This afternoon is the first game for the Summitville Middle School basketball team. Looking at the flyer on her desk, she notices that her honorary position as referee to start the game begins in 10 minutes.

"I'm off to shoot some hoops," she laughs as she passes Darci's desk. "How do you like my outfit?" coaxes Hannah, as she puts on the school cap.

"Don't you look sporty! The kids will love your designer sneakers!" jokes Darci.

Heading towards the back door of the gym, Hannah notices a few members of the basketball team near the entrance to the boys' locker room. She assumes from their loud shouts that there is excitement in the air—and she shoots a smile as she quickly heads toward the players' bench.

She's just about to say to Coach Riley that she's ready to play when they both turn to see two boys in basketball uniforms fighting near the locker room entrance.

She starts to head toward the fight. Stopping her, the coach puts up his hand and states, "Relax, Ma'am; I've got this one."

He then rushes over to separate the boys and end the altercation.

Hannah watches from a distance and sees that one of the boys is sent back to the locker room and the other boy is in tow with the coach. A feeling of doubt comes over her as she wonders if she should go and oversee the situation. Choosing to support her staff's judgment, she stays back.

When she asks the coach what happened, he says that Johnny Richards punched a kid. The coach says that he ordered Johnny to take off his uniform and come back with the locker room aide and sit on the bench for the entire game.

"Are the kids all right?" Hannah asks, concerned about the safety of the boys.

"They're boys—nobody's bleeding," jokes the coach. "We've got a game now. I'll write the report later," he says, looking away from her as he heads toward the court.

The Summitville team players take their positions. As the parents and community members yell and cheer, the coach gives Hannah a signal to come to the center of the court.

Hannah's thoughts flash back to her high school basketball days as she stands in the center ring. She firmly catches the ball from the coach, asks if the teams are ready, and then throws the ball up between the two starters to begin the game.

Hannah climbs up on the bleachers to watch the game. As she sits on the aluminum frame, she sees Johnny Richards coming back to the team's bench dressed in his regular clothes with tears in his eyes. He sits down and looks at no one. She starts thinking about the situation and notices that the kid playing guard is the other kid who was part of the altercation. As she starts to put a name to the face, she realizes that the boy is Ned Wright, son of Regina Wright, the president of the school board. A wave of uneasiness comes over her. She makes a mental note to alert her superintendent.

23
Confusion on the Court

WHEN HANNAH COMES IN THE next morning, the incident report from the coach is on her desk. She reads it and finds that the coach has suspended Johnny Richards from after-school play for two weeks in accordance with the school's Code of Conduct for extra-curricular activities. She looks to see if there is anything written regarding Ned Wright's involvement. Seeing none, she asks Darci to set up an appointment with the coach and to set up separate times with the two boys.

Later that morning, Mrs. Richards, looking quite upset, enters the school and demands to speak to the principal.

Darci barrages her to glean more detail; when satisfied that it is a legitimate request, Darci finally buzzes the principal.

Mrs. Richards enters Hannah's office with an air of determination. She sharply greets Hannah, stating that her child is being unfairly punished and that he did not hit Ned; rather, it was Ned who hit Johnny. She confides in Hannah that her son is a good player and is one of the kids competing for a starting lineup position.

According to Mrs. Richards, this is not the first time that Ned gets away with things.

Listening to Mrs. Richards recount her version of the fight between the two boys, Hannah experiences that uneasy feeling again.

She tells Mrs. Richards, "Thank you for sharing your understanding of what happened. I am still looking into the situation. I will get back to you before the end of the day with more information."

That afternoon, Tom Riley comes to Hannah's office. Hannah greets him at her door. Leaving it open, she asks him to sit down and describe what happened yesterday in the gym.

"I saw Johnny Richards hit Ned Wright. You were just walking in at the time, remember? And, so, I ran over and separated the boys and told Johnny to get in his street clothes and go sit on the bench so he could see the game—and that I would handle him later."

Hannah says, "Are you aware that the boys are giving conflicting statements? I met with both of the boys separately today and both blame the other. All I know at this point is that one of the boys is not telling the truth. How well could you see the situation from where you were?"

Coach Riley says, "I saw it very clearly. It began with Johnny pushing Ned into the wall and giving him several punches."

As Hannah records the coach's statement, she revisits the scene in her mind and wonders how either she or the coach could definitively determine the fault of the incident from where they were standing. "So, according to your account of the scene, you clearly saw Johnny hit Ned several times. Is that correct?"

The coach nods his head and asks if he can go to his class.

"One more question. What was Ned's response? I noticed that you didn't include his name in the write-up. What part did he play in this?"

"None. It was all Johnny's fault, Ma'am."

Before Hannah excuses him, she asks him to sign an amended report, indicating that Ned was the recipient of the punches and that Ned was not part of any wrongdoing.

After initialing the amended report, the coach darts out of the chair and heads out the door, without waiting for her dismissal.

She puts her hand on the phone to call Mrs. Richards and hesitates, as she reluctantly agrees to support her teacher's account of the incident.

Picking up the phone, she dials. "Mrs. Richards? This is Hannah Gardner...."

Outside her office, Frank Amber continues to neatly stack the delivery of copy paper.

24
Never a Typical Day

FRANK AMBER RUSHES DOWN TO the Main office. "Darci, where is Ms. Gardner?"

"She's in her office on the phone—wait, don't disturb her," guards Darci, as she tries to stop Frank from barging into Hannah's office.

"Ms. Gardner, I think you need to come to the art room right away," exclaims Frank, out of breath, as he darts into his boss's office.

"I'll call you right back, Mrs. Wendall," as she puts down the phone. "What is it, Frank?" questions Hannah, seeing him wave to her to follow, as they both bolt down the hallway.

"Ms. Gardner, I am sorry to interrupt you, but Ms. Kent is losing it! She is yelling at the top of her lungs to one of the kids—I don't know what for—but it doesn't feel right."

"Has this ever happened before, Frank?" ask Hannah, as they bound up the second level stairwell.

"Well, it is getting near the Art Festival event—you know, the big one that is part of the Summitville Harvest Gala. She gets easily frustrated around this time, but, today, I am afraid she's lost it."

Hannah arrives at the door of the art room and sees Andy Keller frozen on his stool while Ms. Kent is screaming at him, ripping up his paper.

"What is going on, Ms. Kent?" Hannah asks, as she quickly stands between the student and the teacher.

With a flushed face and a lock of hair flying out from her loosely clipped bun, Ms. Kent flings a paintbrush toward the windows, causing purple paint to splatter onto the pane. "I've had it! These kids are impossible! Andy was suppose to draw a scene from memory—and look what he does!" as she tries to piece the picture together. "I told them not to do any repulsive artwork. These pictures are to show their artistic maturity and the whole community is going to be evaluating them."

"I understand that you always expect amazing work from your students, Ms. Kent," says Hannah in a soft voice, as she attempts to calm the art teacher.

Hannah moves closer to her, gently takes the ripped paper from the trembling hands of the teacher, and gives a directive. "Ms. Kent, why don't you go down to my office. Mr. Amber will escort you and get you a glass of water. I'll stay here with the students for the rest of the period. We'll talk about this in a bit."

Ms. Kent snaps, "No, I have too much work to do. I don't have time to get water—I haven't even eaten today. The Gala is in two days and nobody's helping me."

In a reassuring but authoritative tone, Hannah says calmly, "All will get done; just take a break."

Quietly, Hannah waves Frank in and says in a low voice, "Mr. Amber, can you send Mrs. Caldwell up here and stay with Ms. Kent in my office until I come down."

"Sure," says Frank, as he waits for Ms. Kent to follow him.

"And, Mr. Amber, can you also have some lunch sent to my office for Ms. Kent?"

"Absolutely," says Frank, sensing that the drama is nearing its end.

Mumbling to herself, Ms. Kent stuffs a bunch of projects into her cradled arms. Several start to slip from her grip.

Frank moves quickly toward her. "Here, let me help you, Ms. Kent." Picking up the fallen artwork, Frank escorts the steaming Ms. Kent out of the room.

Hannah looks at the full art class who seem a bit stunned after witnessing such an unusual demonstration of non-professionalism.

Using her body language and a soothing tone to change the atmosphere, she encourages the students to go back to work. With the door open, she motions to Andy to come in the hall and talk with her.

"Are you okay, Andy?"

Andy looks down at the floor in embarrassment. "Yeah, I'm okay. Sorry, Ms. Gardner."

Darci appears around the corner. "Ms. Caldwell, will you please escort Andy down to the office. I would like him to write up what happened today. Also, I need you to find a substitute for Ms. Kent's art classes for the rest of the day. I think she has only two classes left."

Hannah turns to Andy. "Andy, kindly get your books. We'll work this out. Ms. Caldwell will take you to the desk next to hers. Have you had lunch yet?"

Seeing Andy nod his head indicating that he had, Hannah adds, "Okay. Go with Ms. Caldwell. I will be there soon."

At the end of the class, Hannah goes down to the office. She takes Andy's report and carefully reads it. "When did your uncle die?"

"Just last week. Uncle Tony was like the father of our family. I never knew my real father."

"I'm so sorry to hear that, Andy. He must have been very important to you."

"Yes, Ms. Gardner. I feel like I lost my best friend."

"Oh, so sad. When we lose a family member, it takes time to heal. Do any of your teachers know?"

He shakes his head.

"I see. So, no one knows your pain," consoles Hannah. "That is why it is important for all of us to share our feelings with our school family." She continues to read his report. "Were you in class when Ms. Kent told the students what they should draw for the festival?"

"No, I was out most of the week. I got the assignment from my friend. I knew I was suppose to draw something that was part of my memory—and all I could think of was the final scene when I had to shovel dirt on his coffin," tears Andy.

"I'm going to give your mom a call and see if she can come in later. Are you feeling okay to go to your next class?"

"I'm okay, Ms. Gardner. I don't want to miss any more of my math class."

Hannah writes Andy a pass and writes a separate note to Mrs. Lauder, seals the note in an envelope, and asks Andy to give it to his teacher. She shakes Andy's hand and wishes him to have a good afternoon.

Hannah heads into the conference room, where Ms. Kent is cutting out paper frames for the Art Festival displays, obviously more in control of her emotions.

"Can I go back to my classroom now?" asks Ms. Kent in an exasperated voice.

"We need to talk first. What happened today?"

"Do I need my union rep? I've got so much to do—I don't have time for this."

"If you feel you need a union rep, then let's talk 8th period when Mrs. Lauder has a free period. In the meantime, if you like, you can continue to work in this room."

"But I need my stuff from my classroom and I've got to teach my classes."

"Your classes are covered. Tell me what you need and I'll have Frank get them for you."

"Are you holding me hostage? I've got an art show to put on, in case you didn't know," pipes Ms. Kent sarcastically.

Taking a breath, Hannah firmly replies with an authoritative tone, "No, if you need to, you can go home. You have two options: 1) to use the conference room, or 2) to take the rest of the afternoon off. Going back to your classroom is not an option at this time."

With a pause, Ms. Kent says, "I'll use the conference room."

"Good. I will send for Frank and ask him to help you out. I will have Darci ask Mrs. Lauder if she can meet with us 8th period. Would you like me to leave the door opened or closed?"

"Closed; thank you."

With that, Hannah closes the door to her conference room and gives instruction to Darci.

Hannah moves to her office, takes out a banana from her bag, and sits back in her chair. While eating the fruit, she reflects on the afternoon's dynamics. She writes in her notebook: *Stress is a silent enemy to understanding.* She gives Maddy a call to ask if she could stop by his office after school.

25
Dare to Change

AFTER SHARING THE DRAMA OF her day, Maddy smiles at Hannah and says, "Brava. You have just experienced one year in a day. And you're still breathing."

With this comment, Hannah releases lots of emotion in a very hardy laugh. "None of this was taught in Ed Leadership courses." She breathes a long sigh. "Is there a manual for this?" she queries, jokingly.

Maddy chuckles. "It's called experience—oh, and, also, it's called holding onto the words you have been given from the people who have nurtured you. I'd sure like to meet *your* mother!"

Hannah sees his sincerity and says, "My mother? My mother had a very simple background. She was able to look at a situation for what it was—and didn't try to tie other meanings to it. My mom had clarity— she was able to listen with her big heart and her approach to life made people feel comfortable around her. She always acknowledged the best in people. In turn, people would show the best of themselves." With a pause, she says pensively, "A very patient, gracious woman."

"Now I know why you have those traits naturally," acknowledges Maddy, sensing the depth of their conversation. "You know, Hannah, people have different mothers—different experiences—different values. People that work for you need to know your values to be able to be part of your vision. This is one of the most challenging tasks of leadership. As you work toward engaging your staff with a new focus, you approach this undertaking with what I like to call a change of consciousness."

He sees her complex smile and gazes at her with a knowingness. "Change is never easy, no matter how many times you do it. But, realize that change is a constant. How you handled Ms. Kent—by giving her choices, yet standing firm on your values that school is there to nurture the children—opened her reference point, allowing her to remember why she came into education."

Seeing Hannah looking saturated, Maddy responds, "Ah, I see you are wiped out—more on this topic at another time. You've certainly earned another day of leadership. Now, you need to go home and rest."

After she leaves his office, Maddy reflects on his short time left in the district. His daily attempt to communicate with the board members has been a struggle, an undaunted effort to increase the understanding of their roles and responsibilities to the district. Some still hope that McCloud's ways of leading will return. This resistance has stifled the resourcefulness of the administrators. To further support the health and wellbeing of his leadership team, perhaps they would be amenable to another concept. He writes a quick note to himself, closes his desk drawer, and walks over to the coat rack to put on his overcoat.

26
Wright Makes Right

A WEEK LATER HANNAH OVERHEARS Darci commenting to herself that Ned Wright is still on the absentee list. "How long has he been out, Darci?" Hannah asks.

"Ah, let's see. Since last Wednesday. This is Monday." Counting visually on her fingers, Darci says, "Wednesday, Thursday, Friday, Saturday, Sunday, Monday--that's six days. I will give Mrs. Wright a call to see what's going on."

Early next morning, Hannah arrives at school and finds a boy and his mom waiting for her. As she gets closer, she sees that it is Ned and Mrs. Wright. Ned is looking down at the ground and does not acknowledge her greeting.

"We need to speak with you, Ms. Gardner. Do you have a moment or do we need to make an appointment?" asks Mrs. Wright.

Hannah invites them into her office and walks with their pace. She opens the door, hangs up their coats, and offers them to take a seat.

Mrs. Wright begins, "Ms. Gardner, for the past week, Ned has made up one illness after another so he would not have to come to school. Finally, this morning, when I told him that I was taking him to school no matter what, he said that he had to see you first."

"Ned, do you want to talk to me with your mother or by yourself?"

Ned motions his mother out of the room. Hannah asks his mother to wait outside for a moment.

When the door closes, Hannah looks at Ned. "Tell me, Ned; what is troubling you?"

Tears begin to well up in Ned's eyes. "It's my fault; it's my fault," he sobs.

"Are you talking about the fight with Johnny Richards?" she asks, intuitively.

"Yes—I didn't want him to take my spot in the starting lineup. And, besides, I . . . I think he's better than me!"

"What do you mean?"

"I think that the only reason I was a starter last year is because my mom's a board member. And, I was afraid that I wouldn't make the starting cut—and before I knew it, I hit him. But I didn't know he was going to be suspended from the team. That's not fair—and the more I started thinking about it, the worse I felt. I kept thinking about what you said to us this year about character and that your name is only as good as your word. And when I told the coach that Johnny hit me, he believed me, not Johnny." Tears start to roll down his chin. "I'm sorry, Ms. Gardner—and when you asked me, I was just too scared!"

"Thank you, Ned. That took a lot of courage." She gives him a tissue and shakes his other hand. "I am proud of you. Even though it seems painful at first to tell the truth, I have learned that honesty always gives me strength to accomplish whatever I put my mind to."

"Thanks, Ms. Gardner. I actually feel a little better already."

As he throws the tissue in the wastebasket, Hannah says, "Good. Are you now ready to share this with your mom?"

Ned nods nervously.

"Terrific," Hannah smiles. "I will be right here next to you."

She opens her door and asks Mrs. Wright to join them. Hannah opens up the conversation by acknowledging the courageous step Ned made today and asks him to share his story.

When Ned finishes, Mrs. Wright asks her son, "Why didn't you say this right away? Oh, goodness, that explains why you didn't have any appetite this week." She turns back to the principal. "So, what happens next, Ms. Gardner? Is he going to be punished?"

Hannah, sensing the parent's embarrassment and the child's anxiety, simply says, "Mrs. Wright, Ned made a choice today to be honest—though it was a hard one, it was the best one." Hannah looks over to Ned and gives him a smile. "Ned, we will handle this fairly."

A look of relief appears on Ned's face.

Looking back at his mom, Hannah adds, "I will sit down with the coach and the two boys today to put closure on this incident. This is a defining moment for your son and you can be very proud of him."

Hannah stands up to get their coats and warmly says, "Thank you for coming in, Mrs. Wright. I will give you a call later on the outcome. Ned, I will write you a pass for your class."

Mrs. Wright puts on her coat and helps her son arrange his belongings. "Thank you, Ms. Gardner. Here, Ned, here's money for lunch. See you after school." With that, she gives him a hug and walks out of the principal's office with her arm around his shoulder.

Mrs. Wright and her son pass by Darci's desk and say good morning to the secretary on their way out.

After making a pot of coffee, Darci walks into Hannah's office. "Did I just hear Ned admit that he started the fight? Sounds like you have a win."

Hannah looks up from writing her report and smiles, "Darci, what do you have—bionic hearing?"

They both laugh.

"Actually, this one is a win-win for integrity. Thanks for keeping a close eye on the attendance list, Darci."

27
Coach Drops the Ball

LATER THAT AFTERNOON, HANNAH MEETS with the coach and the two boys. Engaging them in sincere and truthful conversation, the boys conclude that each one played a part in the fight. Even though Ned threw the punches, Johnny admits that he said some words earlier that may have fueled the conflict.

With that, they agree that both of them should be benched for the same amount of time. Johnny also says that since Ned had been out of school for a week, that Ned's absences should count toward his time off the bench.

Hannah thanks them both and asks if there is anything that they would like to say to one another. Her eyes glisten as she hears the kind words of apology and promises from each of the boys, as they shake hands.

When the boys leave the room, Hannah asks the coach to stay back. She motions for him to sit back down and begins the conversation.

"I am glad we were able to get to the bottom of this episode. However, we need to talk about one more aspect." She hesitates, letting her voice trail. She then says, "Being a professional means seeing the whole picture without bias. What caused you to excuse Ned from his participation?"

Coach Riley's face flushes.

Hannah anticipates the many choices of answers that could be reeling through his head during the long pause.

Cautiously, the coach replies, "Um, I think you handled today really well. You know, it's all about politics around here," he jokes.

Hannah cringes. She moves forward in her chair and her voice takes on a firm tone. Disapprovingly, she says, "No, Mr. Riley, it's not all about politics—it is, however, all about kids. We are here to give each child the best education possible and to treat each child fairly."

"Seriously, maybe I jumped to conclusions too quickly about those boys," he admits, flippantly.

Hearing his insincerity and knowing that the coach will not take responsibility for his actions, Hannah quickly reminds herself not to get caught in an emotional response. She works to diffuse the energy within herself. Taking a deep breath to calm herself, she turns to the coach and says simply, "I am expecting you to make better decisions in the future."

With that, Hannah stands up and the coach takes his cue to leave.

After he exits her office, Hannah gets a bottle of water and takes a long sip. She reflects back to the day of the fight, regretting that she didn't listen to her instincts.

Moving to her desk, she opens her notebook and writes: *Review staff options with Maddy for near year's coaching positions.*

28
The Dedicated Leader

AT HER REGULAR FRIDAY MEETING with Maddy, Hannah retells the events of the week, highlighting the details of the gains that were made in Character Education. During her recapitulation, another level of awareness occurs within her. A look of distress comes over her as she envisions how the scenario could have gone had Ned not had the courage to come forward and question the coach's motives. Hannah grimaces.

Maddy asks her, "Your voice says one thing—your face says another. What's the matter?"

"I just had a thought—what chance is there that I am missing the bigger picture?"

Maddy pauses and then carefully chooses his words. "Perhaps, you need to just stay focused on being the dedicated leader."

As he sees her eyes widen, he responds, "A dedicated leader is a work in progress. You are on a journey of excellence, being given opportunities for expansion." He gives her a reassuring smile and then calmly says, "So, what is your fear?"

Hannah talks out her concerns with her mentor. She recounts the coach's actions and reactions and wonders if he is undermining her leadership.

Maddy cautiously advises her, stating, "A dedicated leader doesn't get snagged into power struggles. You, yourself, are able to rise above when you feel that there are extraneous agendas. Your focus is on the children that you serve." With that, he hands her the third "C" card that reads: *#3: COMMITMENT: Stay the Course.*

As she takes the card, Maddy continues. "*Caring* and *Changed Consciousness* cannot be manifested without *Commitment*. It is the way to fortify your effectiveness. No matter what the situation, be it politically driven or otherwise, it is most important to remain committed to your values and high ideals, and to uphold an ethical position. It takes courage to do the right thing."

"That is so powerful. How did you come up with these thoughts? Is there a book I can read to find this information?"

He laughs. "Actually, it happens in a heartbeat. You also have it. It has just taken me 43 years of experience to finally be able to articulate it."

She nods graciously. "Thanks. I look forward to seeing you next week."

As he watches Hannah walk down the hall, he rubs his forehead, wishing he could tell her more. *There are some things in this position that never get easier. Confidentiality is a two-way sword.*

29
Three Levels of Consciousness

THE OFFICE FLOOR OF THE gymnasium sparkles as Frank Amber pushes his wet mop back and forth to pick up the daily grime.

The two coaches standing by the bleachers are talking loudly. Tom Riley opens his duffle bag and takes out his car keys, as Jim Aquaceno, the assistant coach, says, "So, you're heading out to your class? Guess you need me to keep an eye on the soccer team for you again."

"Thanks, Jim. The girls are just packing up the equipment. And remember, I'm just in the men's room, if someone asks for me. Don't worry, when I'm principal, I won't forget you covering for me. I'll make sure you get whatever you want." Swinging his athletic bag over his shoulder, the coach waves to the custodian and says, "See you later, Frank."

After Coach Riley shuts the side door, Jim re-tightens the volleyball net for his students, while keeping an eye on the equipment room. One of the volleyballs comes flying towards the custodian. Frank picks it up and Jim walks over to get it.

As Frank hands the ball over, Jim says to him, "Do you think he's just using me, Frank?"

"I try to keep out of these things, Jim. But, let me ask you one question, if I may."

"Go ahead, please. I could use another point of view."

"Well, it appears that the coach is out for the coach. He's an okay guy, don't get me wrong—but he puts too much on your shoulders.

Are you taking on more risk than you realize, covering up for him every time?"

"You're right. How am I supposed to be in two places at once? I'm just the assistant coach. What if somebody finds out? I don't know how to put an end to this."

The respected custodian bends down to release the brake levers and starts pushing in the bleachers. "You're in a tough spot. When I get stuck, I just think about the kids."

"That's good advice, Frank. Got some thinking to do," he replies, as he turns his attention back to the intramurals court with thirty screaming middle-schoolers in play.

30
Homeward Bound

RUSS NEWHART FINISHES HIS LESSON on software coding, addressing how strings can help the developer to quickly assimilate code. He looks up and sees Zack picking up his books, and asks, "Zack, do you have a moment?"

"Sure, Mr. Newhart." Zack walks over to the teacher's lab desk and sets his books near the Bunsen burner.

"Zack, I was wondering if you would be willing to Skype with Jamie Randall and partner with her for the science fair project. Most likely, she's going to be homebound for most of the year. I need a student who has the technical ability and is dependable. You were the first person that came to mind. Is this something you would be willing to do?"

"I don't know. I was hoping to do a really cool project. Jamie might slow me down. I'd have to teach her so much." Zack looks away from his teacher. Taking a deep breath, he responds, pensively, "Is this going to hurt my chances of winning the Science Fair if I don't do it?"

Mr. Newhart smiles and says, "Zack, this town is still talking about the recycled robot you made last year."

Zack frowns. "Yea, but I didn't win—I only came in second."

Mr. Newhart continues. "Zack, I can't imagine anyone slowing down your creativity. Jamie's an A student and a hard worker. I am sure with your combined talents, you will be able to produce an exceptional product."

"And how does Jamie feel about this? Does she have all the equipment to Skype?"

"We will make sure she does. I haven't spoken to her mom yet. I first wanted to make sure we have a competent student who can work with her. If it's okay with you, I will give your mom a call later today to get her permission. Is that okay?" asks Mr. Newhart, looking for confirmation.

"It's okay—but my mom won't be home until 8:00 p.m. I'm going to be late—can you give me a pass to English?"

With that, Mr. Newhart pulls out his pad. "By the way, how is that new iPad doing—you know, the one you won from the contest?"

"Great. It's so much more powerful than my old one. And the kids are looking forward to seeing how the new wristbands work. Thanks, Mr. Newhart," as he takes the pass from Mr. Newhart's hand.

Chapter 4: December

31
The Creative Flow

MR. NEWHART AND ZACK KNOCK on the door and walk into Hannah's office together. Hannah looks up from her paperwork and says, "Looking at your big smiles, what are you two up to now?"

Mr. Newhart enthusiastically explains, "Well, remember how we needed someone to be Jamie Randall's partner for the Science Fair Project? And, of course, Zack came to the rescue. They're Skyping nearly every day and have come up with a great project. I wanted to keep you apprised of their thinking and I brought Zack with me to fill in the details."

"Sounds intriguing. Fire away, Zack," smiles Hannah, as she moves from behind her desk to her new round table, motioning for them to sit down around it.

Zack sets his books on the table and takes a seat. Looking first at Mr. Newhart for assurance, he then speaks to Hannah. "Well, Ms. Gardner, Jamie has really caught the "tech" bug, as we say, and has been learning as fast as she can. Her determination to make this the best science project pushes me to do my best. With our two heads together––(laughing)-–on Skype–(another laugh), we're creating a game similar to geocaching. The idea is to connect and teach software skills to children who are homebound because of their long-term illnesses."

Hannah glances over at Mr. Newhart as she silently acknowledges Zack's precociousness. "Tell me more, Zack."

"Jamie started talking to me about how hard it is to be stuck in a hospital—especially when her brain still functions at top speed but her treatments keep her down. So, then we started talking about other kids in similar situations. You know, it's pretty hard for kids to lose contact with all their friends in an instant, just because of an accident or serious illness. So, we started thinking of ways that we could create a project to help them through the separation and loneliness."

"I like it already," smiles Hannah, as she encourages Zack to keep talking.

He continues. "One afternoon, Jamie said that she had been thinking about the project all day and asked me if I could develop a network that would link kids globally so they can experience a virtual classroom with one another. We talked it out and came up with the idea of a game called 'Tag—You're It' to connect kids to solve geotagging problems using the global positioning system."

"In simple terms, what does that mean?" asks Hannah, looking at her teacher.

Mr. Newhart turns to Hannah, and says, "Zack and Jamie would be developing a database for those who want to take part in the trial run, and then, using ground-breaking GPS techniques, would use a code system that Zack developed to implement the game—which uses latitude and longitude coordinates and search engines—thereby, increasing their mapping skills, problem-solving skills, and critical thinking skills."

"How doable is this?" asks Hannah to both of them.

"According to Zack, very. Zack's coding skill level has even challenged me," smiles Mr. Newhart, looking over at Zack.

Zack gives a quick shoulder shrug, acting as if it is a cinch to complete the project.

Looking back at Hannah, Mr. Newhart continues, "I wanted your okay for this advanced project. This has the potential to be an innovative model for kids to develop their computer science skills while convalescing."

"And are there any concerns about safety regarding these students?" Hannah asks Mr. Newhart.

"No—none that I can see. We have state-of-the-art safeguards in place from the special funding that I got from the PTA technology grant that you helped me get," he answers.

"Well, Zack, it sounds very ambitious and very lofty, I might add," replies Hannah. "Are you sure you can complete this in time for the Science Fair?"

"Yes, Mr. Newhart said he would guide me whenever I need help. And my mom's a software engineer and she knows a lot about databases. That's what she does in her job. So I think we'll be okay."

"Well, there is no question that this project is beyond what we offer in our curriculum, so I would like to have weekly updates," she says to Mr. Newhart.

"Not a problem," agrees Mr. Newhart. "Are we set, young man? Is there anything else you want to say?"

"No—just thanks, Ms. Gardner, for letting Jamie and me do this project. Jamie will be excited."

As the two of them leave her office, Hannah returns to her desk and ponders. Her intuitive sense cautions her that there may be unforeseen ramifications. She makes a note to share this meeting with Maddy later today.

32
Trusting the Wiz

"As you know, Maddy, Zack Zelman, the 8th grade wiz kid, is helping Jamie Randall, the one who's homebound—via Skype. They are now doing their science fair project together and it's pretty advanced. Maddy, have you had any experiences with students developing software programs that connect them beyond the walls of the schools?" questions Hannah, as she takes a chair in Maddy's office.

"You sound concerned. What are you not saying?"

"I am just—perhaps—being a bit over protective."

Hannah relays the summary of Zack and Jamie's assignment to Maddy, including the part where they would be developing a database connecting other homebound children who would take part in their 'Tag—You're It' project.

"They are both competent students so I probably shouldn't worry," says Hannah. "I just was wondering if you had ever encountered similar scenarios or heard of any problems that I should know about."

"Technology is moving so rapidly that it is difficult to fully safeguard students' exposure to risky situations using the Internet. Is that what your concern is?" asks Maddy.

"Exactly. I did check with his technology teacher and he said that Zack's understanding of technology exceeds his own. That concerns me."

Maddy nods. "This seems to be the case in many schools. These kids are natives to technology and often surpass us 'immigrants.' They are on their computers 24/7, exploring the world of cyberspace."

"Then I believe my job is to make sure they are safe. His mom has a Ph.D. in computer science. I spoke to her when we set up the Skyping—so I assume that she is also overseeing his progress at home."

Hannah takes a breath and pauses. She continues. "I'll send her a text message to confirm her vigilance—she seems to respond best that way."

Just then Maddy's phone rings. "Yes, Ellen. You've got the mayor on Line 1? Good." He covers the mouthpiece. "I need to take this one, Hannah. We've been trying to connect all week. Can you excuse me? I'll stop over to see you at your school tomorrow, if that's okay."

Hannah smiles and whispers, "Thanks," to her boss, as Maddy talks into the phone.

33
Seniors' Delight

ON THE FIRST FRIDAY EVENING in December, Hannah circulates around the student cafeteria with a joyful gait, appreciating the detailed decorations that transform the surroundings into a pleasant restaurant atmosphere. The aroma of honey-baked ham and apple pie fills the air. The 8th graders look more like high school seniors in their shirts & ties and skirts & blouses, as they serve their honorable guests. She sees Mrs. Lauder scurrying around, finding students with free hands to seat the next guests, while at the same time, making new arrivals feel welcomed. Hannah moves about the many tables of diners, who are enjoying the camaraderie and good food, and makes her way to Mrs. Lauder.

"What a fabulous turnout, Mrs. Lauder! Our students look like they have waited tables all their lives. You have done a terrific job. What can I do next?"

"So nice of you to ask, Ms. Gardner. I would love an extra hand. Would you mind greeting the guests, while I help out with the servers? That would be great."

"Sure—I can manage that. Everything looks so festive. It looks like everyone is loving the food—and the kids!"

"Yes, I am really pleased how this evening came together. These kids have come a long way. I can't believe that this is the same class that we saw in September. Oops, looks like I am needed elsewhere!" Mrs. Lauder exclaims, as she rushes off to the condiment table where Frank Amber is cleaning up a spill.

Hannah sees the next party coming in with one of them in a wheelchair. Hannah moves some chairs around to accommodate the women.

"Are you the teacher here? This is so kind of you to do this," says the woman in the wheelchair.

"Actually, the teacher in charge is Mrs. Lauder. She is right over there," points Hannah. "I am just the principal."

"Oh, you're the new principal. You're so young. You look like a student yourself," exclaims another senior. "My granddaughter is going here—Emily Raminski. Do you know her?"

"Of course. She's a bright seventh grader who works very hard," replies Hannah, as she helps push the wheelchair closer to the table.

"And she can't wait to be in 8th grade so she can do all these things. I hear that they love the volunteer work that they are doing this year. You've really made a difference for our town."

"Thanks. They are great young adults and I have a wonderful staff. I hope you enjoy your meal," smiles Hannah, as she leaves them in order to help seat the next guests.

Throughout the evening, Hannah overhears a number of the conversations praising the efforts of the children and the school.

Frank Amber comes up to her and says, "You must feel pretty pleased with the turnout."

"I am, Frank, thanks to all your help. I know it is your daughter's birthday tonight. It's cute how the students set up a table just for her so you could be here. Looks like she is having fun," acknowledges Hannah, as they both look over to her table. "How old is she this year?"

"She's eight and now in second grade. She loves the attention from the older kids. I think this worked out better than if we had celebrated at home. I wish her mother could have seen her tonight. She looks so much like her," reveals Frank in a tender tone.

Hearing the sadness in his voice, Hannah replies, "You are such a caring parent, Frank. So sorry your wife is no longer here. I am sure she would be so proud of you."

"Thanks, Ms. Gardner. I know she is one with the universe, but if she were here, I am sure she would be laughing at me!" He chuckles and then sighs. "The hardest times are always the holidays. So, we're going to my sister's house and spend a few days there. Sheila loves her aunt. Excuse me, Ms. Gardner—looks like my help is needed," he quickly says, as he sees the students trying to push paper plates into an overflowing garbage bin.

Later, after the last guests have left for the evening, Hannah assists the students in clearing the tables. She notices the joy in the students' voices as they stack the serving bowls in the dishwasher. She overhears their chatter that brings a smile to her face.

"This was fun. When do we get to do this again? I wonder if they do this in high school."

"Nah—my brother's in high school and he says all they do is study and write papers."

"My brother has no time 'cause he's on the football team."

"Don't forget we have the madrigal concert next Friday night in the Park. Ms. Joyner says to dress warm because it'll be freezing by 10:00 p.m. when we finish. They are going to serve us hot cocoa afterwards and some refreshments."

"Yummmm--I like this volunteer work!"

"Zack, you loafer—are you texting again? Come on and do some real work!"

85

Hannah looks over at the back of the large kitchen and sees Zack on his iPhone. She walks over to him and sees him key in his responses.

Zack looks up and sees Hannah. "I'm texting Jamie, Ms. Gardner. She wants to know what she is missing tonight. I told her that she would have really liked seeing all the grandparents and their friends."

Hannah smiles. "So glad you are keeping her connected. You're a terrific student tutor, Zack. How is she doing?"

"It's been a bad week—she's been sick a lot because of her new treatments. I thought my texting might cheer her up."

Zack looks down at his most recent text from Jamie and shares it with Hannah: "Great job, Zack! It is only by living each moment in the assumption of one's own divinity that an individual can bring his potential into the world."

"Isn't she something! Sometimes I think, Ms. Gardner, that Jamie is really tutoring me. I never realized that doing such a simple task, like serving seniors dinner, would have such an impact on my attitude."

Hannah marvels in agreement, amazed at the wisdom of these teenagers. "I think you will find that being in service is like that, Zack. Bravo for recognizing the simple joys."

Hannah helps him tie up the last bag and gives him a pat on the back. She watches Zack drag the trash bag with his free hand toward the pile that Frank Amber is making.

She hears Mrs. Lauder giving the final approval that all is cleaned up, congratulating them for a job well done. The children hug one another and then rush off toward the front doors to head for home.

Hannah walks towards the entrance with Frank and his daughter. He opens the door and holds it for Hannah. "You know, Ms. Gardner, people say that you are too good to be true. But I have come to know that what you project is actually who you are. You have rekindled the values we used to have in this school. Thank you. May you have a safe journey home."

As she walks to her car, Hannah looks back to watch Frank lock the big doors and warmly grasps his daughter's hand. Unlocking the door of her car, she thinks: *Sweetness comes in many sizes.*

34
Holiday Punch

THE NEXT EVENING, MADDY LETS go of Lilly's arm in front of the palatial steps of a three-story brick colonial home, glistening with colored holiday lights, decorating its four pillars. Maddy loosens his new birthday scarf that his wife just gave him and knocks on the double doors of Sal Montagglio's home, the president of the Summitville Chamber of Commerce.

Mrs. Montagglio opens the doors and greets Maddy and Lilly with a warm smile, as she escorts them in, while an attendant takes their scarves and coats. "So glad you could make it, Dr. Mathews. It's good to meet you, Mrs. Mathews," not recognizing Lilly for her own doctoral status. "Please come in and make yourself comfortable. Sal's in the library, acting as bartender."

Mrs. Montagglio points Maddy in that direction. She takes Lilly by the arm and leads her into the living room. A roaring fire is going in the mammoth fireplace. The room is heavily decorated with holiday ornaments and seasonal wreaths. There are large red bows on every picture and artwork. Lilly is introduced to the other women, dressed in festive attire, sitting on the plush, overstuffed couches and chairs. A woman in a green and red plaid holiday apron offers Lilly some holiday punch.

As Lilly takes the glass, she walks over to a blonde-haired woman in her thirties, standing by the fireplace, who looks a bit overdressed for the occasion, wearing a low cut, red and gold taffeta gown.

"It's a lovely home, isn't it?" states Lilly, trying to engage her into conversation.

"Yes, it is, Mrs. Mathews. You don't know me, but I am Caroline Riley, the coach's wife." She puts her drink in her left hand and shakes Lilly's hand, as a bit of the liquor spills to the floor.

"Nice to meet you, Mrs. Riley. I have never seen you at the games, not that I've been to too many. How long have you lived in Summitville?"

"I've been banned from the games—guess I get too excited—and, of course, with a set of twins and a kid in high school, I'm real busy at home, Ma'am," she responds as she gulps down her drink.

A heavy smell of alcohol fills the space between them. Lilly takes a step back and politely listens to the coach's wife's chatter.

"We've been married for about fifteen years—got married during our first year in college. I'm a Louisiana gal, but Tom's born and raised in this town and knows everybody. I feel like I'm still a newcomer. Say, do you want another drink?" she asks Lilly, as she takes another glass goblet from the server, exchanging an empty one for a full one.

Lilly shakes her head no.

Mrs. Riley sways a bit and grabs onto the mantle. She continues to ramble. "But Tom doesn't understand that—because he's involved in so much. He runs the Recreation Department for the summer, the golf tournament for the town, the football association for the county, the Chamber Relay Runs for the kids, on top of that—his job as soccer coach for the Middle School. Whew!" she takes another gulp. "I hardly ever get to see him."

Lilly smiles as she listens to Caroline Riley brag about her husband. "Sounds like he's really busy. He must be a pretty important guy."

The face of the coach's wife lights up as she stammers, "You, you, you can say that again, Mrs. Mathews. Everyone trusts him. He has keys to all mu—mu—ni—cipal buildings and schools—which says a lot about how much the town loves him." She takes another gulp, nearly finishing the glass. "And we *git* to *git* invited to parties like these," she whispers, pushing into Lilly's space. "These parties are our best times together."

Lilly sees Mrs. Riley's eyes start to fill, sensing an air of depression.

Finishing her drink, the coach's wife continues. "And, he's done so much for charity. Why, he runs the town's Children's Fair. He's in charge of their June Rose Garden Festival and the big Labor Day *Ploat Farade*," she slurs.

Their conversation is interrupted by Regina Wright. "Excuse me, Mrs. Riley. I just need a word with Dr. Mathews."

With that, Mrs. Wright pulls Lilly aside. "Lilly, I just want to tell you that our children are enjoying their school year. Your husband has truly made a difference on our board. He has a way of making everyone feel valued."

"Thank you, Regina. He enjoys his job. He has a wonderful administrative team to work with."

"Yes, I've come to appreciate the new principal. She has the kids thinking in a new direction. Our son seems much happier than our older son did when he was in middle school. These kids really enjoy doing community service."

Lilly nods in agreement as the two women continue their conversation.

"Maddy tells us that you do volunteer work with Hospice. That must be pretty demanding on you, particularly at this time of the year."

Lilly smiles at Mrs. Wright and says, "Well, actually, it's very healing and rewarding—being able to support families through the pain of loss and separation. Helping them move from utter despair to a calming joy is heartwarming."

She watches Mrs. Wright's face to better understand how deeply to take this dialogue. Seeing a person who is open to her words, Lilly continues. "I feel that I need to give back because of all of the love we were given when we lost our son."

Mrs. Wright touches Lilly's arm. "I am so sorry that you had to experience such a tragedy so early in life. What a gift it is for you to be there for others!"

Lilly shares, "I think it was from that experience that I realized how necessary it is to open to a world beyond what our eyes can see."

Their conversation continues by the warmth of the fireplace flames.

In the next room, Maddy accepts a glass of white wine from the gracious host, makes some small talk, and then moves over to the nearest shelf, surveying some of the book titles of the floor-to-ceiling library. Taking a sip, he listens to the light conversation coming from the men near the bar, including comments from some of his board members.

The men hover around Dan Sterling, asking about the best investments for their portfolios. Maddy sees that Tom Riley mixes right in. The talk changes to their hunting stories. With his back turned away from the group, Maddy continues to hear their voices get louder and louder as they boast about their triumphs.

"Tell us, Tom, how did you find that lodge in the mountains? That was the best! It was like something out of the movies. That fully stocked bar with micro beers and the good stuff—Wow! You outdid yourself! And how," the voice lowers, "did you get those girls next door to come over!"

Maddy hears a bunch of belly laughs and turns to see Dan slap Tom Riley on the back. He sees two of his other board members, Pete and Sam, also join in the frivolity. A funny feeling comes over him as he starts to build a checkerboard in his mind. He continues to observe the interaction between his teacher and the board members and wonders about the depth of this kinship.

Dr. Sanjay walks over to Maddy and interrupts his thoughts. "So, I see you're getting an earful as to the real workings of our town. If you were ever on the high school football team, you're in. Intellect, education, ethics—none of these seem to matter."

Maddy is a bit taken aback by the frankness of this impeccably groomed and usually reserved board member.

Dr. Sanjay takes a gulp of his vodka and says, "Oh, I'm sorry. I thought I was just reading your thoughts about the gamesmanship of this town. Pardon me."

On his guard, Maddy comments, "That's an interesting statement you just made. Did you graduate from this town?"

Dr. Sanjay takes another gulp and replies, "Yes, I was the valedictorian of my class—but that doesn't make me part of the 'good old boys' in this town. These guys have a code unto themselves—and are sworn to secrecy, so I have come to understand. Loyalty is everything, regardless of the ramifications."

Seeing an expanded view of the community, Maddy thanks Dr. Sanjay for his candidness, and then politely excuses himself, in order to join the women in the living room.

Searching for Lilly in her elegant emerald silk blouse, Maddy makes his way through rooms filled with sounds of holiday music and the sweet scent of roses, acknowledging the many greetings along the way.

Lilly catches the worn smile pasted on his face and knows that it is time to go. She meets him halfway across the room, puts her arm in his, and introduces him to the women in the room. After a few minutes, she thanks the hostess and asks for their wraps.

35
Intramurals Accident

THE FOLLOWING THURSDAY, FRANK AMBER helps the assistant coach get the volleyball out from under the bleachers, while a group of middle-schoolers wait patiently for the ball to be retrieved. Just then, a redheaded young coed rushes in and yells, "Mr. Aquaceno, Cassie Jenks took a big fall on the soccer field—I think she got hit with a soccer ball and fell backwards, hitting her head. It looks like she is unconscious on the field."

Jim jumps out from behind the bleachers and looks at Frank, who motions him to go, understanding that Frank will take care of the kids.

Frank tells the kids to sit down quietly and wait until their coach gets back.

Jim runs out to the field with the coed. There, he finds the team hovering over Cassie.

"What happened? Forget that—Karyn, get my bag by the door so I can call 911. Amy, see if Nurse Callahan is still here. Elsie, go get some cold wet towels. Stand back, everybody," demands the assistant coach.

Once he gets his bag, Jim tears it open, fumbles for the cell phone, and then dials 911.

The EMT dispatcher answers.

Jim says firmly into the phone, "Send someone to the Middle School soccer field right away. We have a girl unconscious on the field." He touches her wrist. "Yes, she has a pulse and is breathing lightly. They are on their way? Great!"

After disconnecting, he sighs, and knows he has to make the next call. "Darci, is Ms. Gardner right there? Let her know that we have an unconscious kid on the field—Cassie Jenks—Yes, I have called the paramedics—they are on their way. Oh, and tell her I need some backup supervision. Thanks."

As Darci hangs up, her face clouds for a split second. She looks at the clock—3:25 p.m. She guesses that Coach Riley has probably slipped away to his course. Facing a bit of a quandary, she knocks on her boss's door and then barges in and sees her boss on the phone.

Darci interrupts. "That was Jim Aquaceno. He's on the soccer field— Cassie Jenks is out cold. EMT has been called. He says he needs backup."

"I have to go," commands Hannah to the parent on the other line, as she throws the phone back onto the receiver. She immediately rushes out the doorway, toward the field.

She passes Ms. Joyner who has a violin case in her hand and relays the details. Quickly, they both head to the scene, where they now see the paramedics driving onto the field. Jim gives the update and says he needs coverage for the Intramurals court. Hannah gives him a funny look and then asks if Ms. Joyner could stay a few minutes longer and assist.

"No problem," remarks Ms. Joyner. "I was my high school's volleyball queen!" as she rushes off to the gym.

As the EMT personnel strap Cassie onto the stretcher, the young girl starts to come to. The paramedic team members ask her a few questions. A sigh of relief comes from everyone as she gives her name and address.

One of the paramedics states, "We're just going to take her to the Good Samaritan Hospital for observation. She will probably be able to come home in a few hours. Who's got the parent information on this girl?"

As Jim grabs the medical information binder from his bag, Hannah asks, "Where's Coach Riley?"

"He's—not here," stutters the assistant coach, as he nervously hands her the binder.

Hannah grimaces and says, "Stay with these kids while I follow the ambulance. We'll talk about this later."

36
The Kids Deserve Better

HANNAH'S THOUGHTS ARE SPINNING AS she drives into the darken school parking lot. From her car, she sees that she has left her light on in her office. She glances over to the district parking lot and sees that Maddy's car is still there. Even though she spoke with him from the hospital, she feels she needs to meet with him for face-to-face dialogue.

Knocking on his door, she asks, "Do you have a moment?" She leans on the doorway, holding her coat over her arm.

Maddy stands up and shakes her hand. "Sounds like you've had a trying day. How is Cassie doing? Thanks for keeping me informed all along the way."

"Her parents took her home a few minutes ago. They were very grateful for our concern."

Maddy smiles, "It's your empathetic nature that kept them calm. So, how are you feeling?" Seeing the apprehensive look on her face, he motions for her to sit down.

"Exhausted—and disappointed," she confides, relaxing into the chair. "I need to share with you a little background regarding today's events. Are you up for this?"

"Fire away," he says, reassuringly.

Hannah relates the day's incident, starting with Coach Riley's absence on the field, with guarded emotion and deliberate control in her tone. "Today's scenario didn't have to happen. And, it could have been so much worse. A child's life was in danger because of someone's disregard for the responsibilities that were entrusted upon him."

Hannah moves forward in her chair and leans toward the superintendent. "He accepted the position and the additional funds that go with it—yet, he had the audacity to leave his charge to someone else who already had an assignment and then leave the school grounds without permission. He's so arrogant—he thinks he can make up his own rules. While I was in the hospital, I kept thinking about what could have happened, seeing Cassie's parents' anxieties."

Seeing her raw emotions contrary to her normal demeanor, he gently says, "So what do you want to do?"

Hannah stands up and walks calmly over to the window, allowing silence to fill the room. She looks out and sees in the distance the single light coming from her office, helping to crystallize her thoughts.

Turning back to the superintendent, she says calmly with resolution, "This happened on my watch. I know that this is also my responsibility. I only have one real choice and that is to recommend that we take Mr. Riley out of the extra-curricular position," declares Hannah.

In a brief moment of silence, another thought crosses her mind. "Maddy, what is it about him that I don't know that I need to know before I take this action? It seems like people are afraid of him and do whatever he asks. Why did that assistant coach agree to cover for him in the first place?"

Maddy breathes deeply and sits back in his chair, as he makes the choice to disclose some of the pieces of the puzzle. "I know that you're probably not aware of the board's history with Tom Riley, so I will try to help you skirt some of the landmines."

Maddy watches her in earnest as she retakes her chair. "As you know, Tom was born and raised in this town. He's a home boy. His many years of having winning seasons earned him the loyalty from the community. He plays golf with some of the board members on the weekends and has even set up golfing retreats for them. Consequently, he is the favored son. Tom was encouraged by some members of the community to get his school leader certification, so he could run the middle school." Looking at Hannah, he repeats, "Yes, your position."

Hannah's eyes widen, and then nods, like she gets it. She urges Maddy to continue.

"So, there are folks that believe that as soon as he finishes the leadership program, Tom will step into the deserved role." With that, Maddy starts wondering if she has the courage to be fully committed to this job and do what needs to be done.

"Are you telling me that when I take the extracurricular job away from the coach, that I will be sealing my future with this district?"

"It's quite possible, given the politics."

Hannah pensively puts her elbow on the armchair and rests her chin on her palm. "Well, first and foremost, the kids deserve better. I have to do what's right for them. Assuming that you support my recommendation, I will be releasing him from his soccer coaching duties as of tomorrow, awaiting the board's final action."

Noting her dilemma, Maddy says in a consoling manner, "When you are committed to do the right thing, even though it is not the most popular, it can be a lonely road. But you will never have to apologize to anyone, because it is the right thing to do. I'll apprise the board president accordingly. Let's meet in the morning when we're both fresh to develop some strategies."

With a greater understanding, she rises from her chair and says, "Thanks so much for supporting me, Maddy. Now I need to take time to process it all." She picks up her coat, says, "Goodnight," and heads out the door.

Maddy watches Hannah leave the building and drive off. He pulls his coat from the coat hanger in the closet, slips it on, and turns off the lights. As he locks the door of his office, he reminds himself: *The journey of the golden heart has no fear.*

37
Teed Off at Myrtle Beach!

ON THE LAST DAY OF the year, Tom Riley waits in the nippy air for his partner to arrive. Coming out of the clubhouse emerges a well-dressed golfer in a white polo wool jacket, khaki pants, and a grey wool cap. "Good morning, Dan, It's about time you got here!" yells the coach. "We've got the front nine this morning."

"I see you got here bright and early. Just had to grab an extra cup of coffee before being beaten up by you. Jeezes, it's freezing out here!" exclaims teeth-chattering Dan. "Say, how do you and Caroline like your suite?"

"Love it! We overlook the 18th hole. Thanks for the terrific holiday gift."

"No big deal—it's just a perk I was given and couldn't use," smiles Dan. He looks up at the sky's ominous clouds. "I hope you're ready for a quick round of golf. But, you'd better watch it—I had three golf lessons last week with one of Tiger's mentors when we were down in St. Martin."

"St. Martin? You're such a globe trotter—I can't keep up with all your travels. How was the weather?"

"Weather was great. Sun was bright—80 degree temps every day. How was the last week of school? Anything happen while I was away?" asks Dan, teeing up to the first hole.

"You haven't been in touch with the supe yet?"

"No, I escaped phone calls and board packets. I'm still on holiday. What's up?" questions the coach's former high school teammate.

"It wasn't the best of weeks, that's for sure. Hope you don't mind me complaining, but, remember," Tom stops as Dan hits his first shot and watches it stay straight on the fairway, "—remember, how you told me to get my certification this year? Well, I've been doing just that—taking courses after school at the local college. As you know, I got my assistant coach to pick up the Intramurals group that the board wanted this year for the girls who weren't able to make my soccer team. And I need the soccer coaching stipend to help pay for my classes."

Placing his ball on the tee, Tom drives the ball 20 yards beyond his partner's. "My professor takes points off our grades if we are not there on time. So, I have to buzz out a few minutes before the late bus. I have my assistant coach watch the kids so I can get to class on time."

The men climb into the cart to move to their next shot.

"So," Tom continues, "just before the holidays, the principal calls me into her office and says that she is releasing me from my soccer coaching duties for the year. She actually said she's going to have my assistant take my place and the music teacher will teach Intramurals. That is so ridiculous!" exclaims Tom, as they get out of the cart and move toward their balls. "What right does she have to do that? Doesn't she have to go through the board first?"

"Gosh, I'm still on vacation. Haven't even read the latest emails from the superintendent, so I really don't know what's going on. Sounds funny to me," states Dan, as he powers his next shot. "How did this happen?"

"I don't know. She's got something against me. Seems like she's after me. She's always asking for my lesson plans and always stopping by my classes. The last principal had great respect for me and never bothered me at all. He knew I knew how to do my job. And he never would have fired me from one of my coaching positions!"

Obviously upset, Tom's next shot lands in the bunker.

"Hey, this might be my day to beat you!" laughs Dan, watching Tom's last shot. "So, what did she say to you? What was her reason?"

"She says I left my kids unattended. That's not true. I covered all my bases. Jim was taking over for me."

Watching Tom chip out of the bunker, Dan looks perplexed. "Anything else I should know? Everything else okay?"

"Yeah, except I'm not going to have the extra money to go to the Open with you this year." Tom watches his friend hit onto the green. "What can you do to get my job back?"

"I'll talk to the superintendent on Monday morning. Now, you'd better focus or I'm gonna win this hole and you gonna be out a lot more money!"

Chapter 5: January

38
Rising Temperatures in the Frigid Air

MADDY IS ON THE PHONE talking to the town supervisor and sees Dan Sterling standing in the doorway. Finishing up his call, he rises and shakes Dan's hand. "You're up awfully early. Did you already get nine holes in?" ribs Maddy.

Dan takes a seat. "Nope, not in this weather. I just needed to talk to you about something," as he sinks into the cushioned chair.

"What's up, Dan? We missed you at the last board meeting. How was your trip?"

"Trip was great. Got a lot of pointers from the pros and actually have a better game. But it looks like I missed some things that happened while I was gone. I met up with Coach Riley during the week and he filled me in on being let go of coaching the girls' soccer team. What's going on here?" he asks with a bite in his voice.

Surprised by the tone, Maddy takes a breath, and says, "I know you've been busy, but did you get a chance to read last week's board packet yet or any of my emails?"

"Haven't even unpacked my suitcase. What's the story on this? In case you forgot, this is the guy we are grooming for leadership. We don't want to lose him. You got to do something about this and get his job back."

Maddy sits back in his chair and calmly says, "Looks like you're upset about the board's decision. What did Tom tell you?"

"He told me that the new principal got him fired from his coaching position. And you know the board really wants this girls' team to succeed. Why did you put the assistant coach in his place?"

"I'm not sure you have all the facts, Dan. Are you aware that a child got hurt because Tom left the school, leaving kids unattended?" Seeing the puzzled look on Dan's face, he continues. "Yes, looks like he has been doing this on a regular basis. He slips out early and leaves the team unsupervised to go to a college class. He drops his responsibility into the hands of the assistant coach, who is already in the gym, running the Intramurals at the same time."

Seeing the questioning look on Dan's face, Maddy continues, "While the assistant coach was checking on his own kids playing volleyball, Cassie Jenks was hit with a soccer ball, fell backwards, and was knocked unconscious. The EMTs had to come and take her to the hospital."

"Oh, so it was the assistant coach's fault. Sounds like he's the one who should be fired, not Tom," sharply replies Dan.

Sensing the direction that Dan is going, Maddy realizes he has to bring clarity to his board member's perspective, without losing sight of the bigger picture. "Dan, we had a child hurt and it could have been much more serious. What led up to this was a teacher accepting an extra duty during a time when he knew that he already had another obligation."

Dan, still visually angry at the superintendent's rationale, turns his back to blatantly show his disrespect to the elder. He pulls out his vibrating phone from his pocket to read a text message.

Turning back, he says defiantly, "Are you sure you've got your facts, right, Supe? I think the coach sees it another way and will take action if necessary."

Maddy decides to continue in a stronger voice. "Nothing destroys morale more than the acceptance of incompetence and mediocrity. Mr. Riley put his responsibility on another faculty member and never let administration know. This action jeopardizes the well-being of all the students involved and compromises the safety and effectiveness of our school district, to say nothing of the legal issues that could culminate from such an event."

In a range of swirling emotions, Dan stands up, feeling somewhat embarrassed but still defiant. "Well, did you have to take such drastic measures? It's not how we do things around here. We could have worked this out."

Maddy interrupts, rising, and matching Dan's stance. "The board discussed in Executive Session to take this action—you know, the one that you missed—and we voted on it in public session."

Staring right at Maddy, Dan says, confrontationally, "Don't think that this is over—I'm going to talk to some board members."

Maddy opens the door for him. "By the way, where did you meet up with Tom?"

Seeming a bit startled, Dan looks at the door handle, avoiding eye contact. He answers, "On the golf course."

"Last week? Between the flakes?"

`"Ahem, no," he stutters. "We were down at Myrtle Beach."

"I see, just the two of you?"

"No, our wives came too." With that, Dan turns his back to Maddy and walks down the hall with no further comment.

Maddy heads back to his desk and jots a note to himself: *Next meeting with Hannah—Courage and the Big Picture.*

39
Tea with a Twist

As Maddy finishes drying the last dish, Lilly fills the kettle and puts it on the gas burner to heat up the water for their evening tea. Maddy takes his favorite chair in the living room, puts his feet on the ottoman, and glances at the cover stories on the front page of the newspaper, then sets it aside.

Hearing the kettle whistle, Lilly shuts off the stove and makes their brew. She sets his tea with lemon on the side table and relaxes in the chair next to him.

Lilly brings up the repeated question, "So, any word about when the board will hire the new superintendent?"

"Well," he says, grimacing at the topic, "the board is interviewing preliminary candidates in two weeks. It should go quickly, once they complete the process." He takes a sip of tea and changes his tone. "So, what do you want to do after that, my dear?"

Lilly laughs. "How convenient of you to change the subject! You know what I want to do—I want to go somewhere where it's warm." Lilly shivers as she buttons up her sweater. "I know you love this job, but everything has an ending. Knowing you, you'll never take retirement!" She breathes a sigh. "How are things going with the new principal? Is she staying true to her inner core?"

"She's doing great. The kids love her; the parents respect her; and the teachers are starting to come around. The big problem I see, of course, is the board. Dan Sterling came in my office this morning and laid into me about Hannah's recommendation of relieving the coach from his girls' soccer assignment. I found out that he and Tom went to Myrtle Beach over the long weekend—and Dan never shared that with me until today. This coach seems to have his fingers in everything."

"I found out from his wife at the holiday party that he has the keys to everything, too," cautions Lilly.

"Yes, and Dan wanted me to override the board's decision of removing the coach. That's what McCloud would have done. He even thought the assistant coach—you know, the teacher he left in charge with both classes—should be the one removed from the job, not the coach. Ooohh, that left ovary of mine is kicking up again."

They both have a good laugh.

"I know, always trust that left ovary of yours," grins Lilly, with decades of wrinkles outlining her smile. "So what's your next step, Doctor?"

"I'm not sure. Typically, interim superintendents have three choices: they can just sit back and keep things rolling on, as usual. They can be the expert and focus on cost cutting. Or, they can really be effective, improving quality performance, and be the change agent."

"Well, there's no doubt in my mind which choice you're taking— and you have the courage it takes to stay the course. Remember the strength we found together when we lost Ben." Lilly takes a quick breath, then slowly exhales. "Gosh, I am proud to finally say his name without a lump in my throat."

She looks at her husband and holds his hand and says, "But think of what we learned from letting go—allowing the pain—then, the closure when we accepted that his life was on his time—not ours."

He puts his other hand over her hand and slowly adds, "...Giving us clarity of purpose and helping us move forward, together." His eyes water with affection.

The grandfather clock in the hall chimes nine.

"Lil, the district is still dealing with the loss of McCloud and the loss of his leadership, even though folks know it was not ideal. They're experiencing their own bereavement. At one level they're experiencing the loss; at another, they're experiencing change."

Maddy turns and stares at the pendulum. "It takes great patience from the new leadership to keep the organization balanced throughout the mourning period. Often, new ideas get silenced. Folks living in the past are fearful, saying phrases like, 'This is the way we've always done things.' They're not aware of the tremendous opportunities open to them."

Lilly's eyes also follow the swaying movement. She interjects, compassionately, "Their resistant to change stifles their growth."

They both sip their warm tea.

Lilly continues. "You know, in the evolutionary cycle, individuals discard the old while embracing the new: like breathing out and breathing in. Flexibility is critical to survival when moving on the continuum of life."

"There you go, again, dear wife, with your conceptual thinking. Now where are you going with that anthropological mind of yours?"

Collecting her thoughts, she states, "A fearful attitude fosters an impoverished spirit—and closes the door to the heart."

Maddy looks at her with amazement. "If that's true, then my job as a leader is to be the key that unlocks that door...."

He drifts into his own decision-making while taking a final sip of his tea. "...And to expand the organization through kindness, synergistically, moving it towards its lofty goals." He sets the empty cup down and rises from his chair, charged with a clearer understanding of the path he is going to take.

"You're in that daring state, my sweet husband, thinking beyond the norm. As you walk that path, I'll be right by your side." She takes his teacup. "When did you get so smart?"

"When I married you," he flirts, as he turns off the kitchen light.

40

Second Administrators' Retreat: Expanded Leadership Spiral

MADDY ARRIVES EARLY AT THE Chamber of Commerce site and hums a tune while he takes off his gloves and opens the door to the historic building. He pulls back the heavy forest green drapes to allow the glistening sun bathe the room. A quick glance through the windows takes him back to a time when falling snow meant hot chocolate and cinnamon toast.

Looking around the room, he sees wood piled by the fireplace. He opens the flue, rolls up some newspaper, chris-crosses the wood, and lights the fire. When the flames start to rise, and the sound of crackling wood fills the silence, Maddy turns his attention toward staging the room to accommodate the morning's agenda. He pushes the plush green leather chairs around the large conference table.

Soon the administrators fill the room and move toward the inviting fire. After exchanging jokes and laughter about the frigid weather, they take their seats around the solid wood table.

Maddy begins the meeting. "I'm so pleased with the accomplishments we have made since our last retreat. When we met in October, the focus was on sustaining energy. Since you all came bouncing in here this morning, my guess is that you have mastered that goal."

After a hearty laugh and comments by all, Maddy continues. "My goal this morning is to expand your leadership awareness."

The group looks at one another wondering where the interim superintendent is heading.

"Stay with me while I stretch your thinking," he smiles, warmly. "When I turn my attention to that of service, a wealth of understanding—gained from my contemplative thoughts—occurs. It is from this new insight that I guide my staff."

"To build capacity," Maddy continues, "leaders need to experience the world around them by using a wider lens. You may find a model, which I call the *Expanded Leadership Spiral* or ELS for short, helpful. The core of the ELS is when the leader is in sync with his or her higher self—the creative self—and firing on all cylinders, so to speak, allowing insights to be realized."

With this comment, the administrators look perplexed, but knowing their leader's unconventional approach, they try to stay focused on his words.

Sensing their desire to understand the ELS concept, Maddy uses this momentum to build the framework. He continues. "The Expanded Leadership Spiral is a principle to raise the awareness and consciousness of the leader and, ideally, his or her staff."

He walks over to the easel. "To help you better understand this process of expansion, let me present a model for you," says Maddy.

He turns the page that says, "Welcome, Wonderful Administrators!" and uncovers the words on the next page: "What do you know about the *Fibonacci Number Sequence?*"

The members look at one another, hoping to find an answer within the group.

After a few moments, Tim says, "Is that the spiral that keeps expanding based upon a mathematical formula? I seem to recall something about it in my science classes."

"You are right, Tim," acknowledges Maddy. Underneath the words, Maddy writes a series of numbers: "0, 1, 1, 2, 3, 5, 8, 13, 21, 34, ..."

Maddy continues his explanation. "The Fibonacci Number Sequence is a mathematical rule, created by a series of numbers. The sequence is created by adding the last two numbers of the sequence together in order to create the next number, which, when plotted in a circular formation, gives us a spiraling effect. This unique spiral illustrates the perfect harmony and proportion of nature's natural growth pattern. You could have easily read about it in your science classes, Tim. It is found in countless examples, such as in animal horns, seashells, Queen Anne's Lace, and in many other plants and flowers."

"I remember that now," exclaims Bob. "It's pretty awesome."

Maddy flips to the next page on the easel and shows the following diagram:

THE FIBONACCI SPIRAL

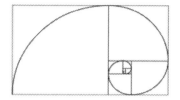

"So what does this have to do with leadership?" Maddy queries, as he looks around the group. The group eagerly searches the new diagram for clues.

Maddy helps them through their discovery. "If you use the formula, you see that the spiral expands, getting bigger and bigger. Let's look at this same graphic another way."

Maddy flips the chart to expose the diagram vertically.

Model: EXPANDED LEADERSHIP SPIRAL (ELS)

Love Supreme
Higher awareness in the present moment of ethical responsibility

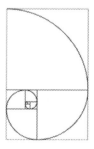

Unaware of the present moment of ethical responsibility

Love Null

"In leadership terms," Maddy says, warmly, "the ever-outward growing shape of the Fibonacci Spiral perfectly traces an expansion of the ethical path we should all be journeying upon." With blue marker, Maddy traces the shape on the second diagram.

"From the spiral's inner center, we begin an ever-expanding pathway of enlightenment. This symbolizes our spiritual growth as we move toward an expansion of consciousness, or what Maslow tried to express in his quest for self-actualization, or what some call *Love Supreme.*"

Maddy continues with new excitement in his voice. "I have found that everyone is somewhere on this spiral. In my experience, as the individual becomes aware of a higher agreement of leadership, the individual connects to a higher ethical standard and radiates from this new energy. These qualities uplift those who follow the leader's direction and assist in cultivating the open-ended spiral."

Maddy pauses as he feels the shift in the room. He looks for a response.

Hannah quietly murmurs, "Are you saying that the purpose of leadership is to bring oneself into a higher consciousness, while also guiding others to their higher self?"

"And that we're always learning exponentially?" adds Bob.

"Yes, excellent. This expanded thinking is usually caught first by those closest to the leader, often called *the inner circle* as well as those who are in daily communication with the leader. They, in turn, carry the new consciousness and influence the organization as it reaps the rewards of a new way of thinking. This makes for a better environment, a kinder workplace, a place conducive to learning. It is the first step in building synergy. As the leader raises his or her awareness, so does the circle, and eventually, the organization."

The administrators slowly nod their heads in agreement as an introspective dialogue simultaneously occurs. They engage in highly charged collegial conversation.

Maddy uncaps his bottled water and takes a sip. He sees a lighter look on their faces as he allows the group to digest their thoughts. "By now, you are understanding how the ethical path strengthens your leadership, never having to apologize for your actions. Are you also aware that living the ethical path gives you the courage to embrace change?"

Their in-depth discussion takes on new vitality as the administrators tell their own stories of how the ethical path was not the easiest. They speak of the courage it takes to do the right thing. They also share stories about leaders whose power was diminished by not following the ethical path.

Minutes fly by as the group starts to understand the impact of this heightened ethical state on their subordinates. The team of administrators bond as they realize how Maddy's symbolic use of the spiral has already been part of their leadership successes. The group appears more confident as they open to a new vocabulary of communicating with one another.

"So how do we keep the ELS synergy going? More on this at a later time," he grins, amusingly.

Carl blurts out, "What? You are going to let us hang out there until the next time?"

Maddy laughs. "The best meals are always savored. Remember, being a leader is a gift," as he gives a kind glance toward Hannah. "Good work for today, folks. Drive home safely."

Chapter 6: February

41
Numbers Don't Add Up

On Monday morning, Helen and Noah Sherman's mom meets with Darci to get the money from the school safe so she can make the deposit from Saturday night's Winter Dance.

Darci opens the safe and pulls out the tin box. Like clockwork, Mrs. Sherman takes the box from her. This mom of twin eighth graders never fails to take her responsibility seriously as treasurer of the Summitville Middle School Booster Club.

"Gosh, Darci, it seems that not many kids attended again. Looks like only about 70 kids showed up. In the past, the number has been more than double this amount. The January dance deposit was even less. Maybe these dances aren't the best class fundraisers anymore."

Hannah walks in from the hall with her observation folder under her arm and overhears the latter part of the conversation. "Is there something the matter, Mrs. Sherman?"

"No. I was just saying to Darci that it seems that the attendance for the dances doesn't seem to be what it used to be. The deposits have been really thin these last two dances."

"How many kids does it look like attended?" asks Hannah.

"Judging from the ticket sales, it seems to be about 70."

"That's interesting. I was there for part of the dance and it looked to be much more than that."

"Well, maybe the kids are sneaking in or something. Anyway, the deposit is only about half of what it used to be," reports Mrs. Sherman, as she recounts the money.

"I'm going to look into it. Thanks always for the incredible job you do, keeping the records accurate and up-to-date, Mrs. Sherman. And thanks," smiles Hannah, "for your commitment to our school."

Hannah walks into her office, pulls out her notebook, and writes: *Mrs. Sherman reports deposit for Winter Dance = 70 kids. Count kids at next dance.*

A thought crosses Hannah's mind. She could use Zack's invention to get an actual head count. She then writes: *Use Zack's student ID attendance wristbands for entering Middle School Spring Dance in April.* With that, she closes her notebook and gazes outside, wondering about the discrepancy.

42
A Midnight Chat on Skype

ZACK TURNS ON SKYPE AND is about to click onto Jamie's name, but then thinks better. Instead, he texts, "Hey, Jamie, are you still up?"

An immediate response comes back to his iPad. "Of course. What are you thinking?"

"I've discovered something. Can we Skype?"

In a few minutes, Jamie's kind face lights up the computer screen, showing her sitting at her desk, completing homework. "Hi, there. So, what's so important? You never call me this late."

Zack clicks on his computer to split the screen. "Look here, Jamie.

See the algorithm we developed? Well, I started fooling with it and found a new way to pattern our ideas. But, I am noticing one thing. It looks like there are 'eyes' following our coordinates. Look here—does it seem like that to you?" Zack asks, as he enlarges the image of concern on his computer screen.

"I am not sure what you mean, Zack. We are just trying to link the kids globally, so they can learn with one another. I see the geotagging connections—Oh, my gosh—I do see something, Zack. What is that ghosting position?"

"You are so smart, Jamie. I knew you would see it, too! I am not sure what this means, but I just wanted to alert you. We may have some unwanted visitors, shall we say. There is nothing they can do at this point, because we're not linking up to a database. I just thought it was interesting. I've been doing some reading on cross-cutting concerns to refactor my coding—so I can move faster and easier—and maybe—as I get more sophisticated in my coding in clone detection and bar codes, I can catch this guy!"

"Zack, you are a genius! You must spend 24 hours a day on that computer! How many other people out there think like you do?" Jamie teases.

"Many, Jamie. Many more than you think. I'm just one little fish swimming in the big sea."

"So glad you know how to swim. Oh, I wanted to tell you that I tested the game today, using the new coordinates you gave me. I think that the kids are going to have so much fun while developing their mapping and problem-solving skills. The hospital dean peeked over my shoulder this afternoon while I was working on it and says she will order a dozen games for the in-hospital school once we finish it," says Jamie, enthusiastically.

"I didn't realize that you have now taken on the job of marketing and sales—touché, Jamie!"

"Well, I was thinking, if we could make some money off this, I could help my parents pay for my medical treatments," prides Jamie.

"Hey, you never know! Miracles happen. Now, listen, I shouldn't be disturbing you at this late hour. I just wanted to get your thoughts to see if I was imagining things. So, off to bed, young lady. I'll talk to you tomorrow afternoon."

"Nice work, Zack. Pleasant dreams."

43

The Mentee Mentors

HANNAH CLOSES THE WOODEN OFFICE door as she motions for Ms. Joyner to take a seat next to her. "I'm sure you have no idea why I asked you to meet with me on a Friday afternoon when everyone else has already headed toward the parking lot."

Ms. Joyner queries as she rests her notebook on her lap, "Are you about to tell me that you are transferring me to another school next year?"

Hannah gives a big chuckle. "Ah, that is not even close. On the contrary, I asked you here first and foremost to thank you for your contributions. Your music program has been instrumental in building student character, not to mention the beautiful music that we have all been privileged to hear in the halls and in the community."

Hannah sets down her cup of coffee that had been warming her hands. "But beyond all of these accolades that many have been saying to you, I want to acknowledge the effect of your sparkling personality, repeatedly uplifting our school."

Hannah sees Ms. Joyner radiate from her kind words and continues. "I love the way you jump in and help everyone, never thinking, 'It's not my job' or 'It's beneath me.' For example, I'm thinking of last week when you helped Frank in the lunch room, when the wind blew over the garbage pails as he was opening up the back doors."

"I was just walking by. It seemed like he needed help," Ms. Joyner explains.

"Yes, and then you magically got all the 8th graders nearby to join in and help him. And then you made them all wash their hands afterwards."

Hannah and Ms. Joyner have a good laugh as they relive the moment.

Hannah regains her focus and says, thoughtfully, "Actually, your impact on our school is much broader. You've earned collegial respect by combining the academics with the arts through your ingenuity and creativity," applauds Hannah. "You've shown that you appreciate the bigger picture."

Hannah takes a moment to let her words settle before she goes on.

Ms. Joyner sits back in her chair, with a shy smile.

Hannah continues, enthusiastically. "The real reason I invited you here today is to propose an idea. You have a natural talent for leadership. Have you ever considered pursuing a career in school administration?"

Ms. Joyner looks surprised. "Wow, I didn't see that coming! I thought you just wanted to ask me to do another concert for the community or something." She pushes a long lock of hair over her shoulder. "I am overwhelmed with your confidence in me."

Shifting more to the edge of her chair, she looks straight at Hannah and says, "I could never do the job you are doing. You have transformed this school in less than a year." She leans forward and whispers, "I wouldn't even know where to begin."

Hannah's eyebrows relax. "Well, you just make the decision to be a leader and then have the courage to act upon it."

"But what if I make mistakes?"

Hannah replies, "We all make mistakes—it goes with the territory. I've certainly made my share, but, with reflection, I learned to center my thinking on what is best for kids. This brings clarity to the real issue and helps me make better decisions."

Ms. Joyner straightens herself in the chair and says, "So, what do I have to do?"

Hannah uses her fingers as a guide to count the steps. "First, you take the certification courses and requirements. You broaden your reading. You reflect upon your internship experiences from the feedback of those who truly care about students. When you become an administrator, your expanded role will help you realize the significance of your new position. It's easy after that."

"Easy? I see you here all hours of the night."

"Well, what does that say about you?"

Ms. Joyner laughs. "You got me there. But, I just love my job and I care about these kids."

"Ah," agrees Hannah with passion. "That's the cornerstone of leadership. I think of my job as the best job in the world. Some days I feel blessed, thinking that I'm actually getting paid for this!"

Ms. Joyner counters. "But there are so many other factors, like working with the parents, the community, some of the less-than-happy teachers—and working with a budget—I have trouble balancing my checkbook!" She pauses. "Actually, I do a pretty good job with my department's budget."

"You do," compliments Hannah.

"This sounds very exciting—especially the way you put it. I'll spend the weekend looking up the Ed Leadership program requirements at the university."

"Terrific!" Hannah gives her a *high-five*. "I also hope to encourage others who want to hone their skills and advance their careers. This collaborative team could be the steering committee for our Professional Learning Community."

"Wow! How do you think of these things?" exclaimed Ms. Joyner, responding to Hannah's conceptual thoughts.

Hannah chuckles. "Sorry that I overwhelmed you. All will come to you in due time. You will have many mentors along the way who will help you gain the knowledge, skills, and confidence that you need."

Seeing Ms. Joyner's enthusiasm, Hannah continues. "Your foundation will always be your love for children."

"I definitely have that! Okay, maybe I can do this!" gleans Ms. Joyner, with a new light of self belief in her eyes, as she rises from her chair.

"Whenever you have questions, you know my door is always open," Hannah reassures her.

As she watches Ms. Joyner head down the hall with a lively gait, Hannah smiles to herself: *Widening the leadership path for others brings joy.*

Chapter 7: March

44
Bully for You

During 7TH period Hannah begins her end-of-the day *walk-throughs*. She stops at Mr. Williams' classroom door, noticing that they have deviated from the English Language Arts lesson on "Red Badge of Courage" to a related topic. From what she is gathering, the students are expressing their concerns about a bullying incident that some of them saw on *YouTube* and questioning how to deal with such a situation.

She's captivated by the discussion from the young students, who obviously have much experience with this subject and are ravishing an opportunity to share their thoughts. Mr. Williams talks to them about letting go of anger and its impact on developing their own character. Students spill out stories of bullying. Their inabilities to resolve their inner conflicts due to emotional immaturity become clear.

As the students' interest on problem-solving with such issues heightens, the discussion intensifies. Mr. Williams sees Hannah at the door and gives her a look of "help" coming from his eyes. Hannah picks up the cue and asks permission to talk to the class.

Taking the role of co-teacher, Hannah asks, "Have any of you lost sleep thinking about a person who kept saying bad things to you or about you or someone else?" Seeing many heads nod, Hannah says, "And yes, females are just as capable of bullying others as males."

"You can say that again," chirps in one of the girls.

Hannah looks at the students who ardently wait for her to continue. "So, let's look into this. When someone is bullying someone, what is that person trying to gain?"

One of the students says, "Power."

Another shouts out, "Control."

Still another says, "I think they do it just to be mean 'cause someone was mean to them."

Hannah agrees, saying, "Like they are justifying their own actions. So, what do these actions say about these people?" asks Hannah.

Student responses start pouring out.

"They want to physically hurt someone."

"They want to make you cry."

"They want revenge for the hurt they are feeling," comes an answer from a student in the back of the room whom Hannah knows is usually very silent and rarely talks in class.

"True," replies Hannah. "We are finding that bullies' actions come from past fears. A major fear is isolation—of being left alone, especially during their early years. Bullies may be reacting to an earlier time in their life when they were neglected. Now, today, they become the center of attention—and they don't care if it is from negative or positive action—as long as it is attention that satisfies their needs."

The students respectfully sit up in their chairs, appreciating the principal's insights.

Hannah moves closer to the students. "That attention can come from their own peer group, from carrying out dares of their friends, or even just the thought of defying authorities. And the bully continues in this addictive role because it gives the bully a feeling of winning."

"So how do we stop the bully?" asks a student in the front row.

Hannah presses on. "Good question. How have any of you stopped a bully before? Let's get some ideas."

One student pipes up, "Punch him in the nose. Stand up for yourself. That's what my dad says."

Another says, "Avoid them at all possibilities."

The quiet student says, "Give no attention to their comments."

"Good start," says Hannah, as Mr. Williams writes their responses on the board. "So let's take each one of these scenarios. What usually happens if you punch the person in the nose?"

"You get into trouble with you, Ms. Gardner," laughs one middle-schooler.

"You get punched back—if not then, then at another time when you're not looking," calls out another.

Hannah grimaces. "Punching or yelling just keeps you engaged in the battle—and the battle continues. You have done nothing to lessen the conflict. The bully is responding to his survival instincts. All you have done is define the territories and most probably, escalated the situation, perhaps getting yourself in trouble with authorities."

"That's not what my dad says. He says, 'If you get hit, hit back twice as hard.'"

"Unfortunately, the old rules don't work—*might does not make right*. You have the tools—and are learning more tools each day. Because you are educated, you have choices. You don't have to lean on your brawn," smiles Hannah, as she flexes her muscle in her right arm and squeezes it with her left, getting a laugh from the kids.

"If we look at the second scenario, which is avoidance," she continues, "sometimes avoiding the situation is a safer way to go. But at times, flight may not be the best answer. When you feel that it is hurting your inner core, you need to do something about it. It's not healthy for you to suppress your feelings. After all, the bully is looking for gratification. Remember, at your age, it is called bullying; at an adult's age, it is called harassment or even assault, depending on the level of contact."

"Let's look at the third choice that was suggested. 'Pay no attention to the comments' is a great way to diffuse the energy of the bully. If you are strong enough to give no attention to the bully's comments, you break the agreement of getting into a win/lose contest, because you are not playing his game. You have no fear," she says with firmness.

"Now, how do you free yourself to move forward in that moment? I can tell you one strategy I have used, depending on the situation," Hannah whispers. She watches the kids lean forward in their chairs to hear her secret. "I ask myself, 'Ten years from now, does this really matter—and am I even going to remember it?'"

The kids laugh, as they think about this simple solution. Questions and comments continue to emerge from the group.

Hannah reminds them that it is their responsibility to report bullying incidents to the proper authority so that the situation can be resolved.

She looks at the clock and realizes that the class time is nearly over. "Listen, I am sorry, Mr. Williams, that we took so much time in your class. It looks like many of your students would like to continue our discussion and come up with more strategies."

An enthusiastic "Yes, definitely," comes from the group.

Hannah looks over to Mr. Williams, who nods in agreement.

"So, what if we take time during lunch tomorrow? You are all invited into the conference room and lunch is on me. And yes, Mr. Williams, if you would like to lead the discussion, that would be great!"

The kids all cheer in excitement, thinking about having lunch with the principal.

Walking down the hall, Hannah thinks to herself: *How can I help these children understand that they are the unique individuality of love's expression and that they are the one, singular source of life? In many ways, they are more awake to their identity of whom they truly are then I was at their age.*

When she gets back to her office, she looks out her window to see the first bus pulling up and thinks: *What a responsibility I have and what a treasure it is to be part of their growth!*

45
Grab the Bull by the Horns

THE FOLLOWING DAY, HANNAH'S CONFERENCE room is filled with kids, submarine sandwiches, bottles of water, and a few teachers, with Mr. Williams at the head of the table. Hannah writes on the Smartboard, "Courageous Solutions to Bullying."

Mr. Williams begins the discussion by summarizing yesterday's class. He states that the purpose of today is to develop strategies to help students through day-to-day disputes and challenges.

Hannah watches the lively interaction. Witnessing the students' enthusiasm and willingness to be vulnerable, she hears their honest thoughts and feels their freedom in expressing their concerns. Her eyes catch Mr. Williams' eyes. He gives her a thumbs up.

Students come up with several ways in securing an anti-bullying environment, including suggesting a student pledge with steps for constructive action.

Nearing the end of the lunch period, Mr. Williams congratulates them for using their Character Education training that has helped move them into a higher level of problem-solving. Looking at the Smartboard, he reads their responses to them:

Courageous Solutions to Bullying

1) **Cool Off**: Have patience and faith in yourself to be able to handle your present emotions to reach your higher self.

2) Follow Your **Emotional Truth**: Give honest feedback on how you are feeling.

3) **Have Courage**: Hear the other person's point of view, without damaging their self–esteem. People are allowed to have their own viewpoints that may differ from yours.

4) **Take Responsibility**: What part did you play in the scenario? What other choices did you have that could have led to a different outcome?

5) **Build a Bridge**: How can you build a bridge between your thinking and the other person's thinking?

6) **Explore Future Solutions**: Believe that change is possible.

7) **Be Gracious**: Focus on the bigger picture. Be willing to forgive yourself and others. Value dignity and self-worth for all. Be grateful for the gifts you were given to become a better person.

One student says, "You forgot one, Mr. Williams." The student looks over at his principal and says, "When all else fails, think "What does this mean in ten years?"

The students laugh as they clean up their lunch areas. Mr. Williams congratulates them all for the great work as the students get their books.

Several students respond. "This was great. When can we meet again?"

Hannah suggests that the next meeting should be with the Student Council and smiles at each of them as they leave the room. Mr. Williams passes by her with a heart-felt look and says, "This was extraordinary. Thank you."

"You are the one who set the stage for this milestone, Mr. Williams. Bravo."

46
Middle School Science Fair

It's Saturday morning and one of the busiest days at Summitville Middle School. Over the years, the Middle School Science Fair weekend event has been instrumental in increasing community support for the school district.

Hannah greets the excited students and their parents as they enter the gymnasium and head toward their projects. She helps a few students reset their displays that didn't survive the active night before.

She signals the evaluating team, made up of high school science teachers, STEM experts from the local businesses, and past winners of the Science Fair, to come together to receive their instructions. They will be using the new, committee-designed rubric, awarding each project with a W-I-N award: a W for Wizard, an I for Innovator, or an N for Novice Scientist with matching ribbons. One project will be chosen to receive the grand prize. The results will be announced at the April assembly.

As Hannah sees students secure their projects, she opens the outside doors for the community members. She then walks around and peruses each project. She comes upon the elaborate display that received so much attention the night before. It consists of two large computer screens: one scrolling, "Kids for the Cure: *Tag—You're It* Connection Game," and the other showing a live link to the Summitville Hospital, with Jamie Randall speaking from her room. On the computer is a webcam, allowing her to see whoever comes to partake in their presentation. Two large audio speakers are at the sides of the monitors. On the display table are brochures of their *Tag—You're It* connection game.

Seeing their school leader stand in front of their project, Jamie and Zack light up with her presence and repeat their presentation to her with full enthusiasm.

Hannah smiles and waves to Zack and to Jamie who is on the screen.

"Ladies and Gentlemen, step right up and see the future of how to conquer the feeling of isolation when distraught by serious illness," chants Jamie like a circus barker, via Skype on the large monitor.

Through their interactive dialogue, Jamie and Zack describe the design and the development of their science project. People start gathering around this innovative endeavor. Jamie and Zack mesmerize their audience as they share their foresight, combining the need for linking homebound children with a state-of-the-art networking system and appropriate data-driven safeguards.

Jamie shares the emotional pain of adolescents with long-term illnesses when they have to stay at home or remain in the hospital for an extended period of time. She talks about the need for this invention.

Zack continues their presentation by describing what technology is currently available and how their project builds upon these concepts. They share their hypothesis on how connecting homebound students hastens the healing process.

Their audience becomes spellbound as the two play the *Tag— You're It* connection game, showing a network database that links kids globally so they can experience a virtual outdoor classroom with one another. Kids solve geotagging problems using the global positioning system, or GPS for short, with latitude and longitude coordinates and search engines.

Jamie reiterates that this game increases their mapping skills, problem-solving skills, and critical thinking skills, while giving them a game to play with other confined children across the planet.

After their ten-minute demonstration, with a much larger group now congregated, the onlookers give a hearty round of applause. Comments abound on the outstanding job that these students have done. Several community members are astonished at the technical level of expertise shown by these two teenagers. Others comment on the students' level of compassion.

After a member of the Summitville Community Council congratulates the two, he leans over to Hannah, querying on how the council can support the school to encourage more endeavors like this.

As Hannah relays her thoughts, she realizes that these two students have helped change the perception of teenage kids in their community; they have become true ambassadors. She smiles inwardly. As she moves toward the next invention, she pulls out her notebook and writes: *Service to others is the great healer.*

47
Power and Pouting

MRS. WRIGHT USHERS THE LOCAL newspaper reporter out of the community boardroom, walks over to close the door and then comes back to the board table to convene the executive session. "We are now opening the executive session to talk about personnel items. On our list is to review tenure and continuing appointment positions. Accepting the recommendations from the superintendent for tenure is one of our most important jobs as board members of this district."

Maddy goes into great detail regarding the teachers who are being strongly recommended by their principals for continued employment. The board has a lively discussion on the quality of the teachers and their portfolios. After 20 minutes, the majority of the board members seem to be in agreement to support the superintendent's recommendations.

Sam Golding has been sitting quietly in his chair and finally speaks up. "There we go again, giving everyone tenure. We're giving them lifetime employment and they only work nine months a year. These teachers make really good money and their day ends at 3:00 p.m. and they never come back after hours. They only take from the community—they never give back!"

"That's not true, Sam. Teachers work long hours into the night and on the weekends grading papers and preparing engaging lessons.

Over the summer they attend professional development courses and seminars to ensure that our students receive a high quality education. And, remember, our teachers come out for parents' nights, the Art Festival, concerts, and are always there to promote school spirit," hails Elizabeth Simpson.

"Yes," interjects Dr. Sanjay, "the eighth graders and teachers are doing a great job, connecting with our senior citizens."

"And just last week the middle school teachers held their annual science fair over the weekend that brought out the entire community. It was the best one ever. Didn't I see you there, Sam?" refutes Mrs. Wright, ignoring Sam's disgruntled look.

Listening to her rebuttal, Dan Sterling's back stiffens as he backs his comrade, Sam. He shrugs her comments off by saying, "Some of us have real jobs—and have to work late."

The three other board members sitting on the left side of Mrs. Wright give sour looks toward Dan.

"Well, I sure hope we're not going to give another year to that middle school principal. We need someone in there who really knows how to handle discipline and how to curtail expenses—she's always feeding people. What are we, a soup kitchen?" he grumbles.

"Now what are you talking about, Dan? The PTA and Booster Club are the ones who supply all the food at those events," states Mrs. Wright.

"Regina, that lady doesn't know how to run her staff—she takes coaching positions away from them after teachers have been doing them for years."

"Dan, we discussed this months ago—get over it," remarks Mrs. Wright, in a frustrated tone.

Setting down his coffee cup, Maddy adjusts himself in the chair. "Madam President, may I share my insights?"

"Please, Maddy, by all means," gratefully replies Mrs. Wright, welcoming his intervention.

Addressing the board, Maddy states, "I've been listening to your perceptions about our educational professionals. I am the one person around this table whom you hired to observe the daily routines and actions of our students and staff," he says, speaking with firmness in his voice. "These past couple months have given me assurance that our school community is hard at work achieving the district's mission. Now, I'd like to share some candid thoughts."

Maddy takes another sip of his coffee. The board members look on quietly to hear what this exemplar superintendent has to say.

"As I recall, you brought me here to help put your house in order."

A few of the board members nod their heads.

Maddy slowly stands and moves behind his chair to elevate the importance of his words. "Building a collegial climate is not an overnight sensation and is never done by just one person. This year I've taken the administrators on several weekend retreats, strengthening the importance of service."

Maddy takes a quick glance around the table, puts his hands on the back of his chair, leans forward toward the group, and calmly continues. "Our discussions focused on the role of the administrative team to fully engage the faculty in their commitment to the success of each student. We developed goals and assessments to evaluate effective teaching that supports a healthy learning environment. Furthermore, our school leaders have committed to model the highest standards and ethics and have pledged that all teachers who will earn tenure must exhibit the same."

Pete fidgets in his chair, admitting, "Gosh, I had no idea that you talked about such things at these meetings. I am so glad that you are taking the time to explain what happens within the schools. Sounds like I have a lot to learn as a board member."

"Thanks, Pete," acknowledges Maddy, as he sits back in his chair. His voice lowers as he talks directly to the newest board member. "Understanding the importance of your role is going to make you a great board member."

Pete sits straighter in his chair, giving renewed attention.

Maddy gives a kindly look to each member. "You now have the detailed files from our leaders who have brought, in earnest, their tenure recommendations to me. You also have read my recommendations for these stellar teachers and for renewing the contract of our outstanding middle school principal."

Mrs. Wright takes the lead. "Has everyone had enough time to review the folders?" Seeing no objections from her colleagues, she responses, "Good." Turning to Maddy, she asks, "Is there anything else you would like us to discuss during this session?"

Maddy realizes that Mrs. Wright is using this moment for him to push the board further, based on their afternoon phone conversation.

He responds, "Yes, there is one more item that I feel would help connect us closer to the community's needs and strengthen the board's effectiveness. How would the board feel about developing a survey–– that is, one where the board asks the community to rate the board's progress?"

"That seems like a waste of time," grumbles Dan.

"On the contrary, Mr. Sterling, we ask our teachers to be accountable—we ask our students to be accountable—why shouldn't we be accountable to our constituents?" Mrs. Wright asks, confirming her leadership role.

"The constituents get to evaluate us every four years—when they vote us in or vote us out," cuts in Sam.

Mrs. Wright shakes her head. "I feel that waiting four years for a community to vote is not acceptable to our growth as a board. Dr. Mathews has given us a stellar suggestion. Each of us cares about better serving our community. It takes courage to hear the truth, even if the response is unpleasant. This would be a wonderful tool for improving the community's perception of our leadership as a board."

"We can lead the way for other community associations," says Dr. Sanjay. "And think of what we could learn. It can only improve our ability to govern, not lessen it," he states with a strong voice.

Elizabeth Simpson adds, enthusiastically, "The Parents in Education forum does this every year. I'd be willing to help develop a draft of a survey."

"And I'll be glad to work with you on it, Elizabeth," jumps in Benjamin Winters.

"That would be great, you two! So, are we ready to go back to public session and vote?" asks Mrs. Wright.

Chapter 8: April

48
The Pledge of Dignity

THE SMELL OF STRONG COFFEE and fresh doughnuts welcomes the staff as they file into the library. One by one, they take their refreshments and a copy of the meeting's agenda. Congenial chatter fills the air.

Hannah greets them as they find a chair. She also shakes the hands of two students who sit down next to Mrs. Lauder. Hannah looks at the clock and sees that it is 3:00 p.m. She promptly begins the meeting.

"Thanks, everyone, for arriving on time to this important meeting. This is a special afternoon for us, as we have two guests representing the Summitville Middle School Student Council. Mrs. Lauder, who has diligently guided the council members all year, is here to share a new initiative that can inspire the best in all of us. At this time, I would like to turn the meeting over to her."

Mrs. Lauder sets down her cup of tea, motions to the two students to join her, and takes Ms. Gardner's spot. "You know, it takes a great deal to make me emotional—but, I have to tell you, a few weeks ago, when the students met to determine how to further the efforts that have been made this year through our school-wide *Leading with Heart* theme, they came up with an idea that moved me to tears. I know we have all seen significant changes in our students this year because of the Character Ed program. But when they said that they wanted the teachers to also show their commitment, I knew we had done a great thing."

"So I stand before you today to introduce Carly Roth, president of the Student Council, and Johnny Richards, student representative of the 8th grade class, to share what the Student Council has come up with to make our school better. Carly and Johnny," encourages Mrs. Lauder, as she motions them to come forward.

Carly awkwardly moves next to her and begins talking. "Hi, everyone," she stumbles.

The adults greet in unison, "Hi, Carly."

Carly responds with a nervous laugh. "Gosh," she says quietly. "Well, here it goes," she continues with a bit more confidence as she opens her sheet of paper. "On behalf of the Student Council, we ask if all the staff and students would take the Pledge of Dignity."

She stops for a brief second and sees Coach Riley entering the back of the library, breaking her train of thought. This interruption makes her hand start to shake. She hands the paper to Johnny, who comes to her rescue.

Johnny continues with a sense of determination in his voice. "So the Student Council came up with the following pledge to be taken by all of us, which Carly will hand out to you," as he motions to Carly to pick up the stack of blue index cards with the pledge printed on them.

When all staff members have their copy, Johnny reads the following, "We, the students and staff of the Summitville Middle School, take this *Pledge of Dignity*:

> I pledge to secure a safe and supportive school community for all, where learning is fun, engaging, and meaningful, where everyone is respected, compassionate, and treated fairly, and where everyone values truth and integrity.

Carly regains her composure. "So, now we are asking you if you would agree to join us in taking this pledge. We thought we could all say it together at the next school assembly. How does this sound?" she asks, as she looks at Mrs. Lauder.

Mrs. Lauder catches the smiles and grins from the staff with several already nodding their heads in agreement. She asks them, "Well, what do you think?"

A spontaneous round of applause captures the thinking of the group. Comments include, "Wow, great job!" and "Such good thoughts!" fill the room.

Mr. Williams stands up. "I make a motion that we accept the *Pledge of Dignity* as read by the Student Council representatives to be read by all of us at the April assembly."

Darci pipes up, "I second it. I think it's fabulous that these kids can be so insightful and sensitive."

Mrs. Lauder says, "Great! Is there any discussion?"

Frank Amber, sitting in the back, overhears a side comment.

"Why don't you just hand over the school to the kids and make them the teachers," grumbles Coach Riley in a low tone under his breath, moving away from the back wall. "We should be focusing on discipline, not democratic rule. I have no time for this! I've got a town meeting to go to."

Also hearing the snide comment, Mr. Conway gives a look of disapproval toward the coach, who is already halfway out the door. He leans over to Frank Amber, sitting next to him, "Personally, I think it's a noble idea."

Frank smiles, as he nods his head and thinks: *Little by little, another jaded voice changes.*

49
Winners All Around!

MADDY SLIPS INTO THE BACK of the auditorium as the Summitville students and teachers file down the aisles and take their seats for the April Assembly. Hannah takes the microphone.

"Welcome, Summitville Middle School students, staff, and parents! This is a wonderful day for our students to gather together to celebrate the accomplishments that they have done all year." Looking directly at the student body, Hannah gives tribute to her students, saying, "I see the brilliance in each of you. You have taken another giant step in creating a successful future for yourself. You are gaining a genuine sense of purpose of who you are and what you can become."

Her following remarks address an appreciation for those who have guided and protected the students along their path of life. She underscores the importance of developing personal values, living by the SMS theme, *Leading with Heart*, and being responsible for good citizenship.

Hannah pulls the microphone away from her chin, motions for students in the wings to come forward and says into the microphone. "At this time, I want to ask Carly Roth and the Student Council members to come forward. They have exemplified student leadership by writing a Pledge of Dignity for all members of our school community. Please give a welcoming hand to your hard-working schoolmates."

Carly takes the microphone as her council members move around her to give her support. Mr. Conway clicks on the LCD projector and the Pledge of Dignity appears on the screen.

"Fellow classmates and teachers, would you please rise to take the Pledge of Dignity," says Carly, in a matter of fact tone.

Hannah smiles as the entire auditorium stands. In the far back corner, the superintendent stands alongside of Frank Ambers.

As the auditorium becomes one voice, there is an electrifying moment.

At the end of the pledge, the teachers applaud the students. Carly thanks everyone for participating in this inaugural moment and states that it is the hope of the Student Council that this pledge becomes part of the opening assembly for every school year.

Moving to the awards part of the assembly, Hannah calls Mr. Newhart forward and asks him to reveal the winners of this year's Science Fair.

Mr. Newhart walks toward the stage and cues Mr. Conway to move to the next screen. "As you know, our Science Fair in March was spectacular. People from all over the county are still raving on the quality and diversity of the innovative projects that were presented. Even Einstein would have been impressed with our stellar inventors and future scientists."

Responding to the quiet laughter in the crowd, he continues. "Producing a quality project requires more than just creating a product. We have worked hard this year to help you build upon your individual strengths as well as your collaborative skills to develop your talents to become future leaders of society."

Mr. Newhart looks around the auditorium and says, "Teamwork becomes essential as a means to expand each member's creativity. All of you have met this challenge at an intense level and because of that, we have W-I-N awards and ribbons for everyone who participated."

Some of the students clap instantaneously, hearing his comment.

"This year we had a very unique situation. One of our entries had to meet the challenge by connecting beyond the school walls. It gives me great pleasure to announce the winning team of this year's Science Fair. Mr. Conway, will you please turn on the monitor?"

Suddenly, in front of the whole school body, Jamie Randall appears on the wide screen wearing the school cap. She is sitting at home at her desk, with her parents around her.

Mr. Newhart announces, "And the Grand Prize winners—with their 'Tag—You're It' social media game for homebound students are: Zack Zelman and Jamie Randall!" As he smiles up at Jamie, he says, "Would you please come forward—You are our winners for this year's contest."

Zack jumps out of his seat and skips up the stairs as the student body applauds with enthusiasm.

Mr. Newhart hands Zack an envelope and tells Jamie's parents to give her the envelope marked "Grand Prize Winner."

Zack looks up at Jamie and sends her an "air" high-five.

Jamie mirrors his response.

Mr. Newhart tells them to carefully open the envelope.

They open it. Each finds a $500 U.S. Savings Bond.

As he watches them smile in delight, Mr. Newhart says, "We want to thank the PTA for supporting this important event. Jamie, would you like to share your experience with your school friends. They can all see you, by the way. Can you see them?"

A loud, unanimous cry erupts from the audience. "Hi, Jamie!"

"Yes, I can see everyone," she giggles, as she waves and they wave back. "Thanks, everybody, for sending me emails, cards, text messages, and keeping me connected. It means more than you know."

Mr. Newhart prompts her to talk more. "What was it like for you, Jamie, to be a part of this project?"

Jamie takes a deep breath. "This science project has been amazing. The Kids for the Cure: *Tag—You're It!* connection game has touched so many people in such a positive way. I never could have imagined that I could be at home and still be part of the science fair, much less winning it. I have to say that Zack deserves all the credit. He is truly a wizard. It was so much fun to work together. Thanks, Zack!" smiles Jamie.

"Zack, is there anything you would like to say?" asks Mr. Newhart. "We would love to know the story of how you mastered the distance connection," as he hands Zack the mike.

Zack pulls the mike close to his chest and quietly says, "I'm not so good at speaking in front of everyone."

He stares at Mr. Newhart, looking like he wants his teacher to take the mike from him. Instead, his teacher coaxes him to keep going. Zack looks up at Jamie.

Encouraging him, she says, "You can do it, Zack."

With that, Zack stumbles for a second, and then says, "I want to thank Mr. Newhart and all the teachers for putting the science fair together. And thanks to the PTA for the Savings Bond."

He stops, thinks for a moment, and says, "There is one more thing I'd like to say. When I was first asked to have Jamie as my partner, I wasn't sure how it would go. I thought she would never be able to get the coding and she would just slow me down."

A laugh comes from Jamie and a few of his peers.

"But she read everything I gave her—and more. Pretty soon, she was getting me to think beyond just the science project—and helped me understand the significance of what we were really doing. When we had our successful pilot connection with other kids, I then realized how important it was to have a great teammate, no matter where *she* is in the world," smiles Zack, looking upward at the monitor. "Thanks, Jamie, you're a true scientist."

Another roar of applause is heard for the winning team. Zack quickly hands the microphone back to Mr. Newhart.

Hannah moves to the center of the stage and congratulates both of them. "I want to also personally thank all the adults. By serving as exemplary role models who give willingly in service, you have given our students a gift for a lifetime."

The award ceremony continues, with each participant coming up on the stage to receive W-I-N ribbons and certificates.

Maddy smiles, gives a nod to Frank, and quietly exits the back of the auditorium, thinking: *Change happens whether we are ready for it or not. Those who keep the heart open are best prepared for the next generation's innovations.*

50
The Grass Is Greener on the Other Side

"MADDY, DO YOU HAVE A minute," asks Hannah, as she knocks on his door with two coffee lattes that she purchased on the way to school. "Here, I think you will need this," she smiles nervously, as she hands one of the lattes to him.

"What's this? Oh, a latte...This sounds serious," he replies, as he takes the coffee from her. "It's only Monday morning. What's up?"

"It's not—bad news. But, I certainly need your input on this one."

"So, let me guess—you've been offered another job for twice the money," Maddy pries.

"Gosh, how do always know everything! Wait, did you hear it first before me?" questions Hannah.

"No, I'm just guessing. I've learned that it's hard to keep good people. If I can get two good years out of stars, I feel I'm lucky. So what are the details?"

"I'll give you the whole story. I got a call on Friday evening at home, asking if I would consider applying for the high school principalship in Bell Ridge. I know it's a great school because I taught there for seven years before taking the assistant principalship in Camel Valley. Looks like they really want me and have already enticed me with a more competitive salary—not quite double," she smiles, "but certainly considerably more."

"So what's holding you back?" Maddy prods.

"That's exactly what I've been wondering all weekend. The offer is appealing, but I'm hesitant—."

Maddy encourages her to keep talking, as he watches her gaze out the window at the early morning sun's rays glowing on the summit. "Hesitant, because?"

"Let me first say that I am so grateful for your guidance and the board's support of renewing my contract. But, before I make any decision, I want to bounce off my thoughts with my mentor. This new offer is great, but there is still so much more work here to do to reach the vision—and I've come to value the people that I work with. We're just becoming a unified voice and the students are starting to feel it. The vision is taking hold and spreading throughout the school community," she says, thoughtfully. "Is this really the right time for me to leave?" she asks as she turns her eyes toward Maddy.

Maddy sits back in his chair, as he takes off the lid to his latte. "Well, the first thing for you to think about is your own growth in this position. Do you feel inspired to come in each day to fight the battles and enjoy the victories? Do you feel that this job allows you to broaden your thinking and stretch your imagination?"

"Definitely. I can say that the professional experiences I have had this year surpass any expectations. Of, course, your guidance has been salient to my growth."

"And now, the job at Bell Ridge. How are you feeling about your ability to expand your skills and knowledge? Are you ready to fight the battles there?" asks Maddy, as he drops the lid into the basket below his desk.

"That is a good question. I've heard that the superintendent is getting grief from his community. Because of the troubles he is having with the new construction project at the elementary school, I am not sure he will have the time to support my lofty ideals," Hannah says with a jovial grin.

"Well, you know I'm not going to be here next year. The board has selected the new superintendent and she seems very impressed with your middle school vision. That's not a guarantee that all will be smooth sailing. But, her reputation and accomplishments underscore her integrity."

Hannah moves more comfortably in her chair while Maddy continues.

"Another thought to consider is where do you feel that you will make the greatest difference? Where is the best match?"

Hannah stares at him, looking for an answer.

"So what do you need from me? To make your decision?" he smiles.

"That would make it easier," she confesses. "What would you do?"

"Ah, this is one time that you have to make your own decision because you are going to have to live your life based upon that choice. Your school theme, *Leading with Heart,* should help your thinking."

Maddy takes a long sip of his latte and continues. "I have learned one thing in my long journey. Actually, I learned it from watching my roses bloom outside my bedroom window. That is, you can never expect something to bloom if you keep uprooting it."

Hannah remains silent as she reflects on his words. Quietly, she gathers her things and rises from her chair. She extends her hand to Maddy and in a reverent tone she says, "Thank you, Dr. Mathews." With that, she walks out of his office in quiet contemplation.

He turns to the window and sees the sun shining on the budding forsythia.

51
Caught Red-Handed

WITH THE 7ᵀᴴ AND 8ᵀᴴ grade Spring Booster Club dance only hours away, Hannah has Frank secure two video cameras to the back wall of the gymnasium. She tries the remote and finds that all is working well.

"This should help keep the kids feeling safer," Hannah smiles at Frank. "Yeah, that's good, Frank. Focus it on the admissions table. That will help us know who's coming in. Perfect. Yes, one on the backdoor, too. Now we have the backdoor and front covered."

At the end of the night, after the coach and the teacher chaperones leave, Hannah asks Frank to come and watch Hannah count the money before she puts the cash box back into the school safe. She quickly recounts the money and finds that it agrees with the coach's tally for the Booster Club. But its total still seems short compared to the attendance. She writes the tally in her notebook, locks the money in the safe, and thanks Frank for staying late.

Uneasy with the discrepancy, Hannah turns on her computer and pulls up the attendance program. 145 kids used their wristbands to get stamped into the dance. She looks at the tally sheet again—only enough money for 87 tickets. What is going on?

Her adrenaline is flowing. She is no longer feeling the fatigue of the late night. Her curiosity leads her right back to the darkened gymnasium. Switching on the master light, she heads toward the maintenance closet, pulls out a ladder, and removes the surveillance DVD from the video cameras.

Turning off the lights and equipment, she heads back to her office and puts the video disc that focused on the admissions' table into her computer. Moving to the track that recorded when the doors opened she watches the kids come in. One by one, the students are scanned by a teacher chaperone; they give their money to the coach; and then their hands are stamped by booster parent volunteers.

Hannah keeps watching. As the number of middle-schoolers coming through the doors picks up, the volunteers at the desk get chatting with each of the kids. All seems quite normal until Hannah notices a new body movement from the coach. She watches intently. It looks like he is taking the money and then grabbing his stomach.

A few more students later, Hannah sees the coach take the students' money. It looks like he is putting it in the cash box, but his arm again goes to his stomach. Hannah pushes the still frame and zooms. The coach's hand is inside his shirt. Hannah clicks the frames manually. She sees a few more students give their money to the coach and then sees the coach's action move from the cash box to his shirt once again.

Hannah hits the stop button and sinks back in her chair. Feeling disgust, she takes a sip of her bottled water and sets it down. She regains composure and dials Maddy's number, despite the late hour.

52
Lunch Ala Carted Away

ON THE LAST WEDNESDAY IN April, Hannah and Darci stroll along the flowered path of newly spouted daffodils that outline the sprawling country club. Finding their way to the executive dining room, they are escorted to their reserved table.

After they order their soup and salads, Hannah hands Darci a card and a little gift box.

"What's this," asks Darci, as she adjusts herself in the plush chair at the Summitville Garden Tearoom.

"Just a little something to honor all of your hard work during our first year together," Hannah smiles.

"But, you've already done enough. As it is, I am the only secretary who has been asked to go to lunch for Administrative Assistant Day," Darci beams, as she graciously accepts the card and gift. "This place is beautiful!" she exclaims, as she admires the elegant surroundings. "Gosh, of all the years I have worked in Summitville, I have never been in this place. Look—there's a bluebird sitting right on the garden water fountain!"

Darci opens her card and focuses on Hannah's handwritten complimentary note. "Thank you, Hannah. I am touched by your recognition."

Hannah smiles. "Truly, I didn't need a special day to notice your ingenuity and dedication. We should have done this much earlier—we just never had time! Now, open your gift."

Darci carefully unwraps the gold-foiled paper and finds a silver and gold gift box. She opens the box and sees a black velvet bag. Pulling apart the drawstring, she discovers a pair of gold-plated daisy-shaped drop earrings with glittering crystals. "Oh, my goodness—these are the Crystal Flower Drop Earrings!" she giggles. "I've been admiring them in the Nordstrom's catalog—they're gorgeous."

"I know," grins Hannah. "I actually 'stole' your catalog book and ordered it from there."

"You didn't!" laughs Darci. "I was wondering where that catalog went!"

"It's inside my top drawer. I promise you can have it when we get back," allays Hannah.

"I have always loved these earrings. Oh, look, they have the lever-back closures. I love these!" gleams Darci, as Hannah watches her put them on. "How did you know to order these?" Darci reaches in her pocketbook to get her compact and takes a quick glance at them. A big smile comes across her face.

"I saw you admiring them one morning and thought that they would be a perfect way to remember the moments that we have shared this year." Hannah moves the paper out of the way as she sees the waiter coming with their soups. "They look amazing on you!"

"Thank you, so much. We certainly have shared a lot this year," Darci states poignantly, as she gently puts the card, earring box, and compact in her pocketbook. "I was just thinking last evening on how different this year is compared to last year at this time. Last year, I felt like a robot—work was not fun. It felt like I was just going through the motions."

Darci touches her new earrings. "And my former bosses rarely asked what I thought—they just sat in their offices and would leave me messages on my email or post-its on my computer, telling me what I had to do."

Darci picks up her soupspoon. "At the time," she says, reticently, while checking her spoon for spots, "I thought that this is the way it was supposed to work because we had so much turnover." She takes a taste of her soup. "This is delicious."

Looking straight at Hannah, Darci puts down her spoon and says, "Can I tell you something? I was actually looking forward to the coach coming into the position. He always stopped by my desk and chatted, making small talk, then would ask to use the other phone. He'd be on my phone playing politics—talking to board members, talking to the mayor, talking to the Chamber of Commerce, while texting on his own cell phone at the same time. I thought he was running for office. Little did I know then what I know now."

Darci leans closer to Hannah and whispers, "When did you first suspect the coach?"

Hannah breathes a sigh. "Honestly, I never did. I think I was as shocked as anyone else. I just knew something was not right." Hannah tips her bowl away from her, takes another sip of her soup, and says, "I actually feel sorry for him—and for our students and staff—and our community as well—for the actions that he took. What happens to one of us affects all of us."

Watching the server take away their empty soup bowls and replace them with colorful walnut and cranberry salads, Darci coaxes Hannah for more information about the coach's downfall. "Did the coach really think that he could get away with it? Mrs. Sherman thinks it's because he felt it was owed to him because he lost his stipend."

Hannah shakes her head. "It is so easy for people to charge others for their shortcomings."

"I still wonder what went through his mind when the police came into the school and handcuffed him. And of all things, he said he felt set-up. How could he claim such a thing, when it was so blatant that he had embezzled funds from the school *and* the town?" queries Darci.

Hannah explains. "It is easy to fall into the trap of one's own thinking—sometimes the competitive nature is a by-product of 'them against me.'"

Hannah stops for a moment, looks at the captivating waterfall, and then turns back. "I have learned that a leadership role sometimes gives one a feeling of self-righteousness—and a justification for one's actions. A little bit of prestige can create a misuse of power."

Darci nods at Hannah's comment. "That seems to be so true. I must admit that sometimes I feel a false sense of power when I sit at my desk and everyone wants my attention. " She grins sheepishly. "It feels pretty good for the moment."

Hannah confides, "You know, it's something that I find I must be aware of all the time. It is humbling to remember that at any time someone else can step into your shoes and the organization would still survive."

Darci quips, "But not do the job as well as you did this year! What's your secret?"

Hannah whispers, "The secret, Darci, is preparing the environment for change."

Hannah sets her fork down and pauses for a moment, reflecting on the coach's demise. "You know, Darci, reality hits in a split second and you realize that you are accountable. Everyone gets what he earns, a direct effect of one's actions; this is the Law of Love."

"That's an interesting way to look at it," comments Darci. "I never thought of it that way. So that's why the assistant coach also had to get a letter in his file. Now it is up to the coach to be honest with himself, so that he can move on."

Hannah replies, "I was reflecting on what you said earlier about your job and how you have come to realize the importance of your position. Now that you've mastered this, what job would you really like to do?"

They engage in an active discussion about Darci's future. When the check comes, Hannah slips cash into the black folder. She helps Darci gather her things.

As they head toward the door, Darci gives her a hug. "Thank you, Hannah, for a time to be treasured."

Catching a last view of the garden, they take a moment to watch five little ducklings follow their mother duck swimming in the pond. Surrounding the fledglings, a group of fully-grown ducks guard the perimeters.

Chapter 9: May

53
Third Administrators' Retreat: Linkage Leadership

ON THE FIRST SATURDAY IN May, Maddy stands at the doorway of the Chamber of Commerce building, holding the door open to help the administrators out of the warm rain. He sees Kristen James getting out of her hybrid car and opening up her umbrella. "Over here, Dr. James," yells Maddy, as a loud clap of thunder echoes in the distance.

They hang up their coats and greet one another, as they head toward the coffee and Danish pastries. Taking their seats around the mahogany conference table, they continue their lively conversations.

Maddy takes his place and welcomes everyone. He re-introduces Dr. Kristen James, their future superintendent, to the group.

After giving a little background of herself, Dr. James asks each of the administrators to share insights of their position as well as tidbits about their personal lives. A relaxed feeling emerges as each one takes the time to share special thoughts with their new boss.

Maddy hands out the agenda and a summary of their past administrative retreats to begin the morning's discussion. "So glad you are able to be here with us during these next two hours, especially at your busiest time of the year, Dr. James. The administrators and I asked you to join us today because we thought you would like to see us in action, as we take the time to value one another's perspective on how we can better serve our school community."

Dr. James smiles, "First of all, please call me Kristen. This is such a pleasure to participate with your team. It truly is a key reason why I accepted the position in this district." She looks around the room. "I look forward to continuing these rich discussions and hope to learn from our conversations today on how to ensure a smooth transition."

"Great. So to bring you up to speed, Dr. James, I mean, Kristen, I will ask our highly-regarded administrators to tell you the concepts we've explored and how they have implemented them to not only improve their leadership capabilities, but also to ignite their schools."

With that, Maddy hands out a piece of paper with two models on it. The first model is the Sustained Energy model, showing how serving others renew the leader's energy. The second model is the Expanded Leadership Spiral (ELS), using the Fibonacci Spiral to show how leading with love grows exponentially.

Immediately, flashes of recognition light up in the administrators' eyes as they pull out their identical fountain pens.

Maddy smiles and says, "I thought this might kindle our conversations with Kristen."

Model: SUSTAINED ENERGY

```
L   10 Good for All (Points to View)
e
a    9                                  Help the community build a playground
d
e    8
r
s    7
h
i    6
p
     5 Good for Some        Take the boys fishing
S
e    4
r
v    3
i
c    2    Go to the gym and work out
e
     1 Good for One (Point of View)
--------------------------------------------------------------------------------
        1    2    3    4    5    6    7    8    9    10
     S u s t a i n e d    E n e r g y
```

Model: EXPANDED LEADERSHIP SPIRAL (ELS)

Love Supreme

Higher awareness in the present moment of ethical responsibility

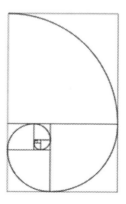

Unaware of the present moment of ethical responsibility

Love Null

Hannah speaks up. "Well, I can talk about the first model," she says, as she points to the graph, "since I was the newcomer at the time. This is the *Sustained Energy* model to help us keep our energies renewed and functioning at optimum efficiency. Dr. Mathews presented this to help us understand how our energies are enhanced when we work for the greater good, the heart of leadership. This model helps us reframe and align our personal goals to our professional goals. In turn, it rekindles our energies to tackle the demanding jobs that we have with a new attitude. I know it really helped me work through the challenges of my first year. Did anyone else feel that way?"

Bob Walton pipes in. "I am the old-timer, Dr. James, and I must admit, that, at first, I had my doubts, but I decided to see if this really works. I had nothing to lose. So, we sat together as colleagues to work on personal goals. Until then, no superintendent had ever asked me about *my* personal professional goals. All I ever knew was that the superintendent's goals were to be my goals. But, this process did two things: 1) it helped me better understand the district's goals, and 2) it allowed me to enhance my leadership capabilities by letting me focus on goals that were important to the success of my school."

Dr. James moves forward to better read Bob's face. "And did you notice any difference in student performance?"

Bob looks at Maddy with a knowing glance. "I have learned that being the right leader encourages right teaching. And right teaching encourages student engagement. This, Dr. James, was the best year of my leadership career. Increased number of Merit scholarship winners, Ivy League acceptances, raised test scores, and extra-curricular participation only tell half the story. We had a camp experience—we worked together—we played together. I think all of us are a bit sorry to see this school year end."

"That's pretty powerful," quietly responds Dr. James.

"Nice job, Hannah and Bob, for leading that discussion. And what about the next model?" prompts Maddy, as he points to the second diagram on the page.

"Pardon me, but, if I'm not mistaken, isn't that the Fibonacci Spiral?" cautiously questions Dr. James. "I recognize it from studying art. But I have never seen it used in a leadership discussion."

"Well, I have never studied art, as you might have guessed," admits Tim Dowling, reminding her that he is the business leader, as the whole group gives a hearty laugh, "but I think I can speak to this one."

"This should be interesting," smiles Dr. James.

"We call the second model the Expanded Leadership Spiral or ELS for short. The leader's purpose," explains Tim, "is to continually have people put their attention on their higher ethical self and to constantly expand and grow in awareness of the higher agreement of leadership."

Carl Irwin adds, "And that focus has a by-product: by being open and accepting, always willing to listen, it allows you to work in a flow—a slipstream, as it will—making your work seem effortless."

"So, if I relate this to art," Dr. James says in a thinking mode, "using the Fibonacci paradigm—as we view a painting, the experience goes beyond the frame. For example, if you are looking at a remarkable painting, such as one by DaVinci, not only do you see the patterns of nature as captured by the artist, your mind takes it further—beyond the frame—and the experience becomes open-ended."

The administrators look at one another and give a knowing smile to each other.

"Seems like you are going to enjoy working with this esteemed team," acknowledges Maddy. "Your comments, Kristen, lead us right to the third and last model that I would like to share with our administrators today—that is, *Linkage Leadership*."

"So, is there a chart for this one?" asks Tim, hearing the thoughts of the others.

"Actually, Tim, this one is harder to illustrate because it goes beyond linear. In picture form, the best example I can give is tossing a rock in the water and watching the waves ripple from the rock's impact. What we don't see is the movement of the water below the surface. This is the power of *Linkage Leadership*."

Maddy takes a more comfortable place in his chair, picks up his coffee cup, takes a sip, then positions his cup to better describe his model. "Actually, using the rock to illustrate the concept of *Linkage Leadership* is just one example." Maddy shifts in his chair. "Let me articulate this in another way."

The administrators lean back in their chairs, ready to capture the wisdom of this sage.

Maddy continues with a slow deliverance. "Links are formed when like-mindedness is established among leaders having a common purpose. In our field, the like-mindedness bonds us together, allowing us to make better decisions to serve as one voice, remembering that it is always 'all about the kids.'"

Tim blurts out loud. "And, as one voice, gives us courage to embrace change."

Bob looks at him with a smile. "Nice, Tim!"

"So, it sounds like *Linkage Leadership* creates a dynamic synergy. Hmmm, that's why leadership teams can be so effective," surmises Dr. James. "And that's why it's so important for leaders to be open to one another. A leader has to trust that another team member may have a different insight, seen through a different lens."

"Absolutely," comments Maddy. "The ability to hear another's point of view gives one the flexibility that erases the competitive nature from problem-solving and supports the greater good."

Maddy looks over to Hannah, noticing her in contemplation. "You obviously are in deep thought, Hannah. "What are you thinking?"

Hannah pauses to put her thoughts in order. She comes to the realization that the Chart of Change: Caring, Changed Consciousness, and Commitment that Maddy shared with her is the foundation of the three models. Thinking about her own dilemma, she responds, "I'm wondering about the importance of longevity on *Linkage Leadership*. What effect do you think longevity plays in the success of your staff?"

Bob Watson quickly responds. "It's key. Seasoned faculty help the new folks join on a higher step of the spiral. Hey, I can't believe that I am finally understanding this!"

"Great insights, you two," acknowledges Maddy, with enthusiasm. "Longevity can promote either an expansion of consciousness or a contraction of ethical responsibility," confirms Maddy.

Maddy looks around his leadership table. Silence fills the room.

Finally, Dr. James speaks up. "My goodness, if this is what your meetings have been like, I don't know how I am going to replace your unique leadership."

Maddy pushes away the compliment, saying, "Dr. James, your graciousness is the link that is needed to carry this district forward. And, you have been blessed with these terrific leaders who are ready to move with you." He rises from his seat and respectively shakes Dr. James's hand. In tandem, the rest of the administrators follow.

As Maddy steps back to absorb the healthy dynamics between the administrators and their new leader, he feels a genuine appreciation for his time at Summitville.

54
FBI Goes Back to School

"DARCI, HAVE YOU BEEN ABLE to get hold of Dr. Zelman yet?" asks Hannah as she cruises by her secretary's desk, handing Darci another annual review to file. "She texted a message on my phone and wanted me to call her."

"No, but you've gotten a few other parent phone calls this morning. And they all sound rather urgent. You might want to give them a call right away. Here's the message from Mrs. Pommery; here's Mrs. Chaisson's; and ah, yes, here's one from Mr. Yi. They've all called within the last 20 minutes and said it's important that you call them immediately. I'm sorry I didn't track you down sooner," she says apologetically, "but I just hung up with Mr. Yi."

The phone rings again.

"Summitville Middle School; Mrs. Caldwell speaking. Yes, Ms. Gardner is here today. May I ask what this is about? Uh-huh. Can I put you on hold for a moment? Yes, I understand. One moment. Thanks." Darci hits the hold button and lays the phone on her desk. "This time it's Mrs. Simpson, yes, the board member, and she also needs to speak with you immediately. What do you want me to do?"

Hannah says, "Let me take this call, Darci. There must be something going on. Give me two seconds to call the superintendent and let him know that something may be up; then I will take Mrs. Simpson's call."

Hannah closes the door in her office, dials Maddy's number, and gets his voice mail. She leaves her short message, and then tells Darci to patch in Mrs. Simpson's call. Within a few seconds of the conversation, the gravity of the situation begins to emerge. The FBI has paid a visit to the families of five 8th grade students, with a concern that somehow they are maligned in a scheme to execute a virus within the state's hospital system. The Hacker Virus Monster, known as HVM1, was discovered by the FBI agents. In the code, the agents found identifiable connections to these kids. A few parents whose kids were best friends with Mark Simpson had already called Mrs. Simpson. They, too, were visited by the FBI this morning.

Darci firmly knocks on her principal's door and interrupts her phone call. "Dr. Mathews is here with two gentlemen. They would like to see you," commands Darci with an intensity in her voice, as she guides the men into Hannah's office and closes the door.

"Excuse me. Can I call you back in a bit, Mrs. Simpson? Dr. Mathews is here to see me." With that, Hannah stands up, hangs up the phone, and ushers the men to sit down. Her heart skips a beat when she registers the serious look in Maddy's eyes. "Dr. Mathews, gentlemen, what can I do for you?"

"Hannah, I would like to introduce you to Agents Ramoz and Anderson, from the U.S. Department of the Federal Bureau of Investigation. They need some information from us."

Over the course of the next twenty minutes, Hannah learns that the FBI has discovered a link between some of her students in the middle school to a malevolent plot that interjects a virus having the potential to corrupt financial information on hospital computers across the state. This act of sabotage, given the name of HVM1, has been stopped with the help of an unknown person, whom they are still trying to identify.

It has come to light that somehow her students are personally involved. Hannah is given a list with six names and is asked what she knows about the character of each one. A lump forms in her throat when she sees Zack's name on the list. A flashback to conversations with the technology teacher drains the color from her face.

55
Phishing Tackled

AS ZACK PULLS HIS COMFORTER up from the floor of his room and sprawls across his bed, his mind reels from the dynamic day. He reflects on the drama of the meetings he had throughout the day with his mom, his mom's lawyer, the principal, the superintendent, and the FBI and their tech guys; something that he never imagined that could happen from just his tooling around with his computer.

It had been so nerve-racking, that, for once, Zack actually appreciated his mom checking up on him before bed, seeing if he was okay. Still a bit on edge, Zack gets out of bed, gets his iPhone and punches in Jamie's number.

"Hey, Jamie. So sorry to bother you—are you sleeping?"

"How could I sleep, Zack, wondering how you are doing? What time did you finish with the guys from the FBI?"

"About an hour ago. They wanted me to share all of my coding, all of the formulas that I developed, and also our database. They took my computers and iPad with them. The only thing they left me with was my phone. They even took the displays we made for our science project!" says Zack in an exasperated tone.

"Wow! I've been home all day, just hearing bits and pieces from my mom. I guess the FBI wanted to come here, but I heard my mom tell the principal that I just had my last treatment and asked if they could wait a day or two before talking to me. I tried to text you a few times today, but my text didn't go through. I thought maybe they had shut off your phone. Hey, I see you have a different number! Tell me all that happened."

"Yes, they took my phone, reconfigured it, gave me my contacts of just my family and friends, and wiped out everything else. I didn't have time to call you. I wasn't going to call you because it's late, but I just couldn't sleep. So, where should I start?"

"I want to hear everything. Start from the beginning," begs Jamie.

"Well, I was in English class, when Ms. Gardner comes to the door and asks me to get all my belongings and come to her office. I thought somebody had died or something. She told me that there were some men from the U.S. government who wanted to talk to me."

"Once we got to her office, I saw my mom and our attorney there. Looks like they had already been talking. My mom's face looked like she had seen a ghost. As soon as she saw me, she jumped up and gave me a big hug—in public! Now, I really thought someone had died."

Jamie laughs. "Oh, come on. Your mom adores you."

"I know, but... Anyway, these G-men wanted to know exactly how I knew so much about coding. I told them that it really started when

I was about three years old and my mom gave me my first computer. I made the G-men laugh, Jamie!"

"But it's true, Zack! We all know that you were born coding."

"Then I shared with them that I wanted to learn more about identifying cryptic coding using Open Source's free intelligence gathering technology to stop computer viruses. So, I told them that last summer my mom enrolled me in an independent college course on the Internet. There were several levels and I qualified for the expert level in program coding and developing new software. I learned how to track the origin of codes and to see trails of data. Soon I discovered a way to protect systems from corruption while developing databases."

"And that's how you were able to develop the database for our geotagging game," reminds Jamie.

"Correct, Jamie. But, remember the night I called you and said that there was something weird going on? Well, I went back to my computer and kept searching until I found a source. At first I had no idea what I found. I knew that it was numbers and names and I thought of it as just a game with someone wanting to join in."

"But just last night, I saw something that disturbed me. It looked like some of those names had tags already on them. As I was following their tags, I started to think that something more serious was going on. Seeing that it could be a virus, I put in a protection code first and then I added code to trap it. I told the G-men that I was going to work on it more tonight to understand what was happening, but—well, all I can tell you, Jamie, is that those G-men work fast!"

"Wow!" exclaims Jamie. "Can you believe our little science project got so much attention?"

"So then they had a meeting with just my mom and the lawyer. After about 20 minutes, they asked me to come back in the office. The G-men then thanked me for my work and said that my links may be able to help crack the case that they have been working on. My mom asked me if I would like to help the FBI. So, I spent the entire afternoon and evening in my home with the FBI as I led them through the maze. I showed them how we created our game; that by geotagging, we were able to apply location coordinates to digital objects, such as photographs and other documents, for the purpose of creating map overlays."

"Didn't they already know how to do that?" asks Jamie.

"Yes, the guys I worked with understood my reasoning and told me that the hackers often used digital photograph records and fingerprinting to give authenticity to their site. What the hackers usually do is manipulate the record of service by changing bar codes and redirecting the compensation funds, transferring them to another account. Once the FBI saw my coding, they realized that the hackers must have tagged onto our pilot so that they could break into hospital databases of patients with long-term illnesses to falsify records and collect government funding."

"So, did this all happen because of our project?" asks Jamie with concern in her voice.

"Actually, this has been happening for quite some time, long before we started our project. The FBI has discovered a virus that allows hackers access to patient information. Each time the patient goes into the hospital for treatments, the hackers are able to steal the profile and sell the list of different bar codes to hackers in Eastern Europe for a sizable profit. This is an international espionage ring. The hackers are careful not to leave a trail."

"But I still don't understand why our project was so important," queries Jamie.

"Unfortunately for the hackers, Jamie, they thought that I was one of them."

56
Small Town Heroes

At the May executive session of the board, Maddy is asked to summarize the HVM1 saga of the past week. By now, everyone in the quiet little town of Summitville has learned about the genius of Zachary Zelman through the mass media sitting on his doorstep.

"Seems like we have a "Steven Jobs-like" 8th grader who has the expertise of a technology guru. Looks like he has been working through Open Source, a source of free technology, to stop the spread of damaging viruses. He learned specific coding while taking a college course on the Internet. While surfing, he came upon the brain code for HVM1. By adding additional code without being detected, he encapsulated the virus, and literally, stopped the effectiveness and execution of it, long enough for the FBI to jump in. Unfortunately, for a few of our kids, they were also questioned because Zack had designed a program that linked them together to share their tweets. Last week Zack was being cast as a villain. Today, Zack has become a hero, not only in his friends' eyes, but in the eyes of the whole nation."

After answering many of the questions pertaining to the details of the case, Maddy looks over to the president of the board. "Well, Mrs. Wright, shall we return to public session for the next order of business?"

With that, Regina Wright adjourns the executive session. The board reconvenes to the public session where they are greeted by a full house of more than two dozen teachers; many middle school parents; several middle school students; and a sea of evening news reporters and photographers.

Zack and Jamie are sitting in the front row with their parents. Hannah, sitting at the far right of the board table, gives them a smile.

"It is great to see that people come out for wonderful noteworthy things that happen in our school. I am sure you are not all here to talk about the summer roofing project that is also on the agenda,"

Regina Wright smiles, along with the soft laughter. "We are here to recognize an extraordinary student—and the remarkable supporting efforts, exemplifying the talents and ethical folks that we have in Summitville. FBI Special Agents Ramoz and Anderson are here to make a presentation and I will hand the mike over to them."

Special Agent Ramoz takes the mike, introduces his partner and recounts their positions. "Most of our day you will find us sitting behind our computer desks. However, every once in a while we have a special moment, such as tonight, to recognize outstanding citizens who have made a significant difference in America. I would like Zachary Zelman to come forward."

Jamie looks over to Zack with a smile, encouraging him to stand up.

Zack shuffles to the microphone.

"Zachary Zelman, on behalf of the Federal Bureau of Investigation, we would like to honor your ingenuity and courage as you partnered with us to uncover a potential threat that could have had serious consequences."

Special Agent Anderson hands Zack his medal and certificate. "Zackary Zelman, on behalf of the President of the United States, we would like to make you an honorary special student agent of the FBI, as recognized by this pin," as he attaches a special pin onto Zack's shirt.

Jamie beams as she applauses with the rest of the audience.

"And," says Special Agent Ramos, "we have one more person that needs to be recognized. Would Jamie Randall please come forward?"

Jamie looks a bit confused, as if the wrong name was said, then sees Zack's hand motioning her to come forward. She slowly stands, shaking a bit.

"We were told by Zack that, while this young lady was convalescing, she had the creative ideas that led to the geotagging game which eventually became the gateway to catching the organized illegal gang. So, Jamie Randall, on behalf of the President of the United States, it gives me great pleasure to make you an honorary special student agent of the FBI, as recognized by this pin," as he attaches a special pin onto her collar.

Jamie looks over to Zack and sees him grinning from ear to ear. She gives him a big smile, and he, in turn, gives her a wink. She turns to see her parents standing, along with the rest of the audience, clapping in loud approval.

Mrs. Wright thanks the agents, shakes Zack's and Jamie's hands, and reaches back for the mike, as cameras flash. "Zack and Jamie, what you have done is beyond the scope of most of us sitting here. This effort is truly remarkable and the board would like to recognize your strong characters by installing in the front hall a plaque called the *Pledge of Dignity*, with your names being first on the plaque. It is our hope that other students will be honored in the future for outstanding service." With that, she shows them the plaque.

The clapping subsides while the two students return to their seats next to their parents.

Mrs. Wright continues. "As this is our last board meeting of the year, the Summitville Board of Education would also like to acknowledge the work of our exceptional educational leaders."

"Ms. Gardner," says Mrs. Wright, "on behalf of the board, and from my own personal experience, we wish to honor you with this plaque that represents our sincere thanks for your courage in putting our children first. Your calm and caring approach with your staff and students is instrumental in making this a banner year for the Summitville Middle School."

Hannah comes forward, accepts the plaque with a bit of surprise on her face, as she shoots a glimpse over to Maddy, seeing him smiling and applauding. Her "thank you" to Mrs. Wright is barely audible as she extends her warm hand. She takes the plaque and looks out to her staff and students, standing on their feet. Her eyes catch Mr. Conway's eyes as he gives her a thankful smile and she sees Ms. Joyner give her a thumb's up. She also sees Cassie Jenks and her parents waving in the back row, as she gives a smile of appreciation to the crowd and takes a seat.

Mrs. Wright then asks her vice president to come forward and help with recognizing the outstanding work that the interim superintendent has done in bringing change to the Summitville school community. As the vice president holds the microphone, Mrs. Wright reads the board's statement that hails Maddy's character.

Maddy graciously accepts the kind remarks. The board quickly passes the consent agenda, confirms the date of the summer reorganization meeting, and then makes a motion to adjourn the meeting.

Afterwards, Mrs. Randall comes up to Hannah and says, "Congratulations, Ms. Gardner. You certainly deserve this special recognition. I also want you to know that we have one more thing to celebrate. We just came back from Jamie's doctor—she's been given the 'green light' and should be able to come back to school in the fall."

A broad smile instantly comes across Hannah's face. "Oh, my gosh, Mrs. Randall! I am thrilled with this glorious news. You must feel relieved. You have done so much to make sure that Jamie got the best of everything to triumph throughout this whole ordeal!"

With that, Hannah gives Mrs. Randall a big hug and shakes Mr. Randall's hand. "You can count on me to do all that I can to make Jamie's entry into high school a smooth transition."

Hannah gives accolades to Jamie. Taking her hand, Hannah whispers, "Jamie, you are so beautiful in strength and character. I am proud of you for pulling through a tough year with honors."

Jamie whispers back. "Ms. Gardner, there are no mistakes in life. This was an amazing year for me. I know why I am here and why you are too. Everything is always perfect."

At first, Hannah is stunned by the perception of this young soul, then, instantly remembers Jamie's text to Zack at the Senior Citizen dinner. With that, she gives Jamie a hug, realizing that her leadership role in the education of children has to embrace this new paradigm of consciousness.

Zack and his mom come over to join them; together, they walk toward the main door. Patricia Zelman shakes Hannah's hand and pulls her aside.

"Thanks, Ms. Gardner, for all you have done to improve the self-esteem of these two kids. There's one more thing you should know about their successes. Just before we left the house tonight, the Randalls got a call from a toy company telling them that they want to meet with Zack and Jamie to see if they could market their game," says Dr. Zelman. "Looks like Jamie is quite the marketeer. We wanted you to know, but we haven't told the kids yet. The Randalls didn't want this news to take away from this evening's special honor. We'll share the news with them tomorrow after school."

"Wow, that is sensational, Dr. Zelman! They have worked so well together to make the world a better place. You have to be so proud of your son."

The two rejoin the other parents and kids surrounding Zack and Jamie, who now resemble celebrities, rather than the two humble kids that they are, and the group departs for the evening.

57
Service With a Hook

AFTER THE BOARD MEETING, MANY of the board members come over to Maddy and shake his hand, wishing him well in his retirement years. The board president talks to him for several minutes. She gives him her final goodbyes and heads toward one of the camera crews near the front door. Maddy picks up his leather binder, steps back from the table, and watches the room in celebration. A warm smile comes over his face as he walks over to answer the news reporters' questions, most probably for the final time in this district.

As the last of the public audience leaves and the reporters close their notebooks, Maddy glances at the big clock on the wall and realizes that this was the shortest board meeting of the year. He picks up his gait, exits the building, and happily moves toward his car in the school parking lot. There, by Maddy's driver's door, he sees Dan Sterling pacing around in a circle.

"What's up, Dan?" asks Maddy, hoping to diffuse the angry energy that he senses.

Obviously fuming, Dan's reddened face and ears are a give-away as he kicks around the circle of pebbles he has created with his foot in the parking lot. He looks directly at the interim superintendent and speaks rashly. "I've been on this board for 18 years. You've been in this district for nine months. I've given my whole life to this community. My judgment was never questioned. You, on the other hand, have the nerve to come here and bring your academic ideals, disrupting the balance of our board."

Dan's body language looks like he wants to punch Maddy out.

Maddy takes a calm step backwards. "Dan, I'm sorry that you didn't get re-elected to the board. Don't take it personally. Change is inevitable. And there are so many other ways to serve the community," counsels Maddy in a reverent tone.

Dan winces. "There you go again. You're always acting like the preacher. I don't know what power you have over these other lackeys, but you don't fool me!" yells Dan, with a flushed face.

"What is really bothering you, Dan?" asks Maddy in a steady, soothing voice.

"What is really bothering me! You've forced our best coach to have to revert to other means 'cause you took his livelihood away—you let that principal destroy his career!"

Maddy searches for the words to say without getting dragged into the argument. "I hear your concern about the coach." He pauses, and then asks, "Is that what's really troubling you, Dan?"

Dan moves toward his own car. He leans one arm on the side view mirror for support. Suddenly, Dan gets very quiet.

Maddy sees Dan start to tremble and senses his desperation.

"Are you okay, Dan?" he asks, as he steps closer to Dan's car.

Dan whips around. "You don't know the half of it," he snorts. "This defeat has ruined my family. Seems that my support of the coach has made the community turn against us. My wife's so upset, she wants to leave this town." Dan starts to choke up. He stares at the school. "I've given so much. This is the only place I've ever lived," he stammers weakly, "and some of my best clients have started to pull their portfolios from me."

Maddy speaks softly to console him. "Look, first of all, you are not to blame for the coach's demise. You are not responsible for someone else's character flaws. I am sure that the coach will recompense for his actions and move forward in his life, perhaps not working in schools, but somehow making use of his coaching talents. And, as for you," Maddy smiles warmly at him, as he feels Dan re-gaining composure, "people forgive and forget in time. Go home and give your wife a big hug."

Maddy watches Dan sink quietly into the driver's seat.

After Dan drives off, Maddy slowly walks back to his car. He hears voices in the distance, turns, and sees Frank Amber helping the Randalls getting Jamie comfortably into their car. Maddy smiles and thinks: *Service without a hook, that is, without expectation for a reward, is done with the heart.*

58
A Year to Remember

LILLY HEARS THE FAMILIAR HUMMING as she sweeps the flour dust from the kitchen floor. "So, how did it go?" she asks with interest, putting away the broom in the closet. "I am sure they recognized your leadership."

Maddy throws his briefcase on the couch, grabs Lilly by the waist, and twirls her around. As her face turns flush, he gives her a peck on the cheek and says, "Oh, Lilly, you would have been so proud! The place was packed. The middle school teachers and parents must have found out that the board was going to recognize Hannah and her students."

Lilly feels the jubilation in his voice. "Ah, so the mentor is elated by the success of his mentee!" She escorts him lovingly to the kitchen table and pours chamomile tea in his favorite cup. "Tell me everything," she begs, as she takes a seat next to him.

Maddy stirs a bit of honey into his tea and sips it. "First off, after the board approved my tenure and continuing employment recommendations, the FBI recognized Zack Zelman for his amazing discovery and said some wonderful words. It was so special! Camera crews were everywhere. There wasn't a dry eye in the place. That kid is already getting offers from MIT and CalTech! And he's such a humble kid—that girl he tutored is equally gifted and they recognized her, too. What a great team they made!"

Lilly beams. "How fortunate for you to be part of their future!"

He takes another sip. "And then Mrs. Wright stood up to make the board presentations and gave Hannah the plaque. At that point, the whole audience jumped up in appreciation. One of the teachers came forward and read a lovely statement recognizing Hannah for her commitment to make a positive change on the Summitville Middle School. Many students were also present, showing their love."

"That is so beautiful, Honey. And what kind words did they give you at the end?" Lilly asks as she passes Maddy a canister of freshly baked shortbread cookies.

Reaching into the tin to get a cookie, he says in a nonchalant manner, "They said all the wonderful words that they always say at the end." He takes a bite of the sweet.

"And...?" she prods.

"Mrs. Wright came up to me afterwards and said that she is a better board president from my guidance." He throws a knowing glance to Lilly. "She understands that boards have two functions: one is the day-to-day work needed for teaching the students of today, and the second is to prepare for the evolving consciousness of our students."

"...Linking the divinity of one generation to the next," grins Lilly.

Maddy takes another bite of the sweet and puts the lid on the canister. "Lilly, one more thing. When I got to the parking lot, Dan Sterling was standing by my car. He was furious and not only did he blame me for not getting re-elected, but he also blamed me for the loss of his status, his income, and his power in the community. I'm surprised he didn't also blame me for how many kids he has."

Lilly chuckles with his analogy and says, "So, how did you handle it?"

"Well, I tried to get to the root of the problem."

"Good. . . and?"

"He couldn't face his own choice—that he backed the wrong horse. When he finally realized that ethics count, it was too late—simple as that."

"And how did you leave him?"

"I tried to practice the law of non-interference. I left him with his own thoughts."

"Okay. . ." she questions. "And did you remind him that we have a choice—that we either change or get left behind—and that this is his opportunity to turn the corner?"

Maddy grabs her hand, knowing he can't leave it there. "I have learned from you, Lil, the art of balance, while you patiently love me, accept me, no matter what." He looks at her face glowing with unconditional love. "All right, I'll call him up next week and ask him if he wants to go to lunch."

Lilly smiles, realizing that he understands not only her words, but also the bigger picture. "Wonderful. Sounds like you have completed the job that needed to be done. What's next? Perhaps our cross-country tour? Or is there something else on your horizons that I don't know about?" she prods with a twinkle in her eyes.

"Nothing that I know of. Guess it's time to get out those travel brochures."

"That sounds adventurous!" she says, excitedly, as she gently takes his arm and helps him rise to his feet. She leans toward him and whispers, "No matter what, you know I will always support you. Come on, let's head for bed," she says, as she turns off the kitchen light.

59
Student Mastery

ZACK CLEARS A SPOT ON his dresser and proudly displays his medal and certificate. Removing his pin, he takes a closer look at it and polishes it. He attaches the pin to his backpack, securing it firmly. Falling back onto his bed, the only word he can mutter is, "Wow!"

Elation is all he can feel. He starts to reflect on the whole experience. Suddenly, he needs to talk. Jumping up for his phone to call Jamie, Zack puts in his password, and sees that he has a text from her. He touches her name on his screen and sees her almost immediately.

"Are you as excited as I am?" asks Jamie, not even waiting for his greeting. "How are you handling this? I can't even think about sleeping ever again!"

"I know how you feel. I am wide-awake, too! Gosh, do you realize that we have been recognized by the President of the United States for our little science project!" Zack gives an infectious laugh, almost to the point of being giddy.

Jamie joins in the giddiness. Hardly able to talk, she chokes out, "And to think, we were almost arrested! Instead, we were awarded with medals!"

Zack, still laughing, says, "It's all so surreal, Jamie. How did we do it?"

Jamie's look becomes more thoughtful. "Well, we began with like-mindedness. We made an agreement and didn't allow judgment of any kind to interfere with our passion. Our idea was born totally from intuition—and, of course, your brilliance."

"Wait—It was your diamond consciousness that was always shining somewhere. Throughout the entire experience, it gave clarity every step of the way. You made it all feel so easy," compliments Zack.

"Wow, Zack! You are becoming quite the philosopher," laughs Jamie. "You were the one who was interfacing with the world, while I was the one in isolation. That allowed me the silence to think, feel, and act from the end, not of the end."

"And that thinking led us right into analysis," states Zack, as he opens up a bottle of water. "It allowed me to focus my attention."

"You're right. I think that once you felt the creative rhythm, you had determination and perseverance, without pushing, to break down and take apart the components to better understand how to build our dream without the fear of failure," critiques Jamie.

"What do you do—sit up all night with Socrates!" he jokes.

Laughing, Jamie responds, "Cute, Zack. And your sense of humor carried me through the tough times."

"Hey, no one would ever believe that this geek has a sense of humor! You're the only one who appreciates this side of me," he jests.

Arguing, Jamie says, "Don't be so sure of that, Zack. I'm sure others find your wit refreshing. I know I have enjoyed the ride all the way."

Silence comes over the phone as Zack sits down at his desk.

"Jamie, I'm still amazed at how the synthesis of our thinking—two polarizing approaches, one that is more cerebral and the other that is more spiritual—could work together to make the sum greater than the parts."

"Me too. I find it amazing that we were able to bring together our two strengths to make a better world."

"Perhaps we are the new matrix of creativity for our generation," announces Zack.

"And a new paradigm for breaking into the awareness of a higher truth," gleans Jamie.

"Ah! That's what separates the common man from the genius," proclaims Zack. Seeing the weariness in her face, he glances at the clock, remembering her recovery. "Now that we have mastered our first challenge, it's time for you to get some shut-eye so we can get on with the next. Good night, Jamie."

"Pleasant dreams, Zack. Talk to you tomorrow."

60
The Path of the Golden Heart

HANNAH KNOCKS ON THE OAK door to Maddy's office to thank her mentor one last time.

He welcomes her in and shares some final thoughts. "You have all the gifts, now, and last night you received confirmation of your accepted leadership here at Summitville. Also, for your information, I just received a phone call. Looks like Coach Riley has accepted a plea bargain and will be serving some time at Lincolnville, but not as an Athletic Director, if you know what I mean."

"Oh, my. I guess stealing from the town's Rec Department sealed his fate," she says, as she sets her briefcase on a chair. "When did you know that the coach was not the best fit for leading the middle school?"

Catching her sincere look, he answers, "When I caught him standing outside your assembly on the first day. I knew he wasn't in service with a genuine heart."

Maddy picks up the picture of his wife on his desk, wraps it in newspaper, and carefully sets it into the box. "You will find that your main challenge now will be how to continue the momentum of success. Ah, but that is another chapter, which I am sure you will write in your dissertation. Now, I need to pack my things and move out of here by 3:00 p.m. so Frank can vacuum and have it ready for the new superintendent."

"Maddy, I will never be able to thank you in words for all that you have given me."

Maddy stops his packing for a moment. "Life is full of beginnings and endings." He takes the picture of his son in his hand, studies it for a brief moment, and then wraps the newspaper carefully around it.

Hannah pulls out an item from her briefcase. "Do you think that you have room in that box for a gift from me?"

With that, Hannah gives Maddy a present wrapped in elegant, silver foil with white grosgrain ribbon. The outside note simply says, "To a master who lives the Golden Age of Education."

Maddy unwraps the gift to find a Waterford Crystal Eagle. The sunlight from the window cascades through the prism and creates dazzling rays that bounce on the walls in the room.

"My goodness, this is so heavy," exclaims Maddy, as he holds it up to the window to view its clarity. "This is a most gracious gift," he says, as he studies its wings. "The eagle symbolizes higher consciousness. Wonderful. I will treasure it always and be reminded of your leadership," he says softly, as his eyes sparkle like the prism.

A few moments pass while he admires the intricate artwork.

Placing it carefully on his desk, Maddy says, "I also have a gift for you."

He opens his desk drawer and pulls out a worn Tiffany box and hands it to her. "It was given to me by my first superintendent when I was a principal. I take it out at times when I need to connect to the reason why I went into this revered profession. I want to pass it on to you now."

Hannah lifts off the cover. There, wrapped in white tissue, frayed with age, she finds a cobalt blue paperweight, in the shape of a heart. She picks it up. Rubbing it with her fingers, she senses its years of service. "He must have been an incredible leader."

"That he was. You have now earned it. Take it with you and let it be a reminder of all the talks we have shared. If you look under the cushion, you will find a meaningful note."

Hannah lifts up the cushion to discover a tattered folded piece of paper. She carefully unfolds it to find the words, "Lead with patience, humility, and love for the greater good."

"This says it all," remarks Hannah. "A most treasured gift. Thank you." She gently places the paper back under the cushion, sets the heart inside the box, and secures the gift into her briefcase.

Turning back to him, she asks, "What are your plans, now that you are finished here? Are you going to take another interim position?"

"Well, actually, I thought I would just take some time to relax and enjoy my retirement. I still haven't had time to do that, you know."

They both laugh at the reality of his statement.

Suddenly, Hannah eyes begin to fill.

"Now, no reason for tears—those who have taken the time to really know each other may be separated by distance, but not by heart. When they reconnect, they engage in conversation as if no time has elapsed. You have my number—and now, I happen to know that your staff needs you so they can give you their congratulations for an extraordinary year—and are looking forward to the next year, I might add," he smiles kindly.

With that, Hannah gives Maddy a warm hug. Picking up her briefcase, she slowly turns and walks out his office door.

As he hears her heels in the distance, he ponders about his next chapter in life, now that his service is over in this position. A melancholy moment starts to overcome him as he continues to pack his books and personal items.

Just then, the phone rings. He picks it up. "Lester Mathews here. Yes, I am. Uh huh….yes; of course I know who you are, Dean Sheffield. Uh huh…Really. A position—to teach school leadership. . . ."

Down the hall, Frank Amber whistles under his breath, as he wipes the glass clean on the outer office door.

Glossary

The 3 Cs -- Chart of Change*

Step 1: CARING: The First Step in Transforming an Organization. (Unfreezing: Discovering the reason for change)

Step 2: CHANGED CONSCIOUSNESS: Courage to Accept a Conscious Change. (Change: Implementation of choice)

Step 3: COMMITMENT: Stay the Course. (Refreezing: Flexibility and follow-through to embrace the new)

Leadership Models**

Model 1: SUSTAINED ENERGY: Service the Greater Good.

Sustained Energy demonstrates how our energies are enhanced when we work for the greater good, the heart of leadership. Energies are renewed and functioning at optimum efficiency when personal goals and professional goals are aligned for service.

Model 2: EXPANDED LEADERSHIP SPIRAL (ELS): Influence Exponentially.

ELS demonstrates the leader's purpose to continually focus attention on the ethical self, expanding the awareness from a higher agreement of leadership.

Model 3: LINKAGE LEADERSHIP: Cultivate Leadership Excellence, Connecting to the Next Generation.

Linkage Leadership creates a dynamic synergy when like-mindedness for serving the greater good is established among leaders. The linkage fosters candidness, courage, and creativity to embrace change.

****

*A practical application of Lewin's Change Theory. Hammond, J. & Senor, R., 2014. The mentor. Bloomington, IN: iUniverse Publishing, Inc.

**Three models for advancing leadership. Hammond, J. & Senor, R., 2014. The mentor. Bloomington, IN: iUniverse Publishing, Inc.

Selected References

Blanchard, K. & Bowles, S. (1998). Gung Ho! New York, NY: William Morrow and Company.

Bolman, L. G., & Deal, T. E. (2004). *Reframing organizations: Artistry, choice and leadership.* San Francisco, CA: Jossey-Bass.

Borgatti, S. P., & Molina, J. L. (2003). Ethical and strategic issues in organizational network analysis. *Journal of Applied Behavioral Science,* 39(3), 337-349.

Chance, P. L. (2009). *Introduction to educational leadership and organizational behavior* (2nd ed.). Larchmont, NY: Eye on Education.

Cremin, L. A. (1961). *The transformation of the school: Progressivism in American education, 1876-1957.* New York, NY: Alfred A Knopf.

Cuban, L. (2008). *Frogs into princes: Writings on school reform.* New York, NY: Teachers College Press.

Davis, S., Darling-Hammond, L., LaPointe, M., & Meyerson, D. (2005). *School leadership study: Developing successful principals.* Stanford, CA: Stanford Educational Leadership Institute.

Drucker, P. F. (1954). *The practice of management.* New York, NY: Harper and Row.

Drucker, P. F. (1966). *The effective executive.* New York, NY: Harper and Row.

Drucker. P. F. (1999). *Management challenges for the 21st century.* New York, NY: Harper Collins Publishers.

Fayol, H. (1949). *General and industrial management.* (C. Storrs, Trans.). London, England: Pitman.

French, J., & Raven, B. H. (1959). The bases of social power. In D. Cartwright (Ed.), *Studies in social power* (pp. 150-167). Ann Arbor, MI: University of Michigan, Institute for Social Research.

Fullan, M. (2001). *Leading in a culture of change.* San Francisco, CA: Jossey Bass.

Getzels, J. W., & Guba, E. G. (1957). Social behavior and the administrative process. *School Review, 65*(12), 423-441.

Gardner, H. (1991). *The unschooled mind: How children think and schools should teach.* New York, NY: Basic Books.

Goodlad, J. I. (1984). *A place called school: Prospects for the future.* New York, NY: McGraw-Hill Book Company.

Goodlad, J. I., Soder, R., & Sirotnik, K. A. (Eds.). (1990). *The moral dimensions of teaching.* San Francisco, CA: Jossey-Bass Publishers.

Hallinger, P., & Heck, R. H. (1996). Reassessing the principal's role in school effectiveness. A review of the empirical research. *Educational Administration Quarterly, 32*(1), 5-44.

Hargreaves, A. (1994). *Changing teachers, changing times.* New York, NY: Teachers College Press.

House, R. J., & Aditya, R. N. (1997). The social scientific study of leadership: Quo vadis? *Journal of Management, 23*(3), 409-473.

Kouzes, J., & Posner, B. (2007). *Leadership Challenges.* San Francisco, CA: Jossey-Bass.

Lewin K. (1943). Defining the "Field at a Given Time." *Psychological Review.* 50: 292-310. Republished in *Resolving Social Conflicts & Field*

Theory in Social Science, Washington, D.C.: American Psychological Association, 1997.

Lin, N. (2001). *Social capital: A theory of social structures and action.* New York, NY: Cambridge University Press.

Louis, K. S., Dretzke, B., & Wahlstrom, K. (2010). How does leadership affect student achievement? Results from a national US survey. *School Effectiveness and School Improvement, 21*, 315-336.

Machiavelli, N. (1908). *The Prince.* (W. K. Marriot, Trans.) Constitution Society. Retrieved from http://www.constitution.org/mac/prince00.htm.

Manz, C. C., & Sims, H. P. (1987). Leading workers to lead themselves: The external leadership of self-managing work teams. *Administrative Science Quarterly, 32*, 106-128.

Maslow, A. (1943). A theory of human motivation. *Psychological Review*, 50, 370-396.

Mintzberg, H. (1983). *Power in and around organizations.* Englewood Cliffs, NJ: Prentice-Hall.

Moolenaar, N. M., Daly, A. J., & Sleegers, J. C. (2010). Occupying the principal position: Examining relationships between transformational leadership, social network position, and schools innovative climate. Education Administration Quarterly, *46*(623). doi: 10.1177/0013161X10378689

Murphy, J. (2006). A new view of leadership. *Journal of Staff Development, 27*(3), 51-52, 64.

Ravitch, D. (2010). *The death and life of the great American school system: How testing and choice are undermining education.* New York, NY: Basic Books.

Roscigno, V., Lopez, S., and Hodson, R. (2009). "Supervisory bullying, status inequalities and organizational context," *Social Forces*, 87(3).

Schlechty, P. C. (1990). *Schools for the twenty-first century: Leadership imperatives for educational reform.* San Francisco, CA: Jossey-Bass Publishers.

Senge, P. M. (1990). *The fifth discipline: The art and practice of the learning organization.* New York, NY: Doubleday.

Sharp, W. L., & Walter, J. K. (1997). *School administrators' perceptions of trends, issues, and responsibilities relating to the modern educational climate.* Paper presented at the Annual Meeting of the Mid-Western Educational Research Association, Chicago, IL.

Stewart, T. A. (2002). *The wealth of knowledge: Intellectual capital and the twenty-first century organization.* London, England: Nicholas Brealey Publishing Limited.

Thompson, J. D. (1967). *Organizations in action.* New York, NY: McGraw-Hill.

Tomlinson, H. (2004). *Education Management: Major Themes in Education.* New York, NY: Taylor & Francis.

Tyack, D. (1974). *The one best system: A history of American urban education.* Cambridge, MA: Harvard University Press.

Tyack, D., & Cuban, L. (1995). *Tinkering Toward Utopia: A century of public school reform.* Cambridge, MA: Harvard University Press.

Weber, M. (1947). *The theory of social and economic organization.* (A. Henderson & T. Parsons, Trans.). New York, NY: The Free Press.

Yukl, G. (1998). *Leadership in organizations* (4th ed.). Englewood Cliffs, NJ: Prentice Hall.

Jan Hammond is an associate professor at Long Island University's Department of Educational Leadership and professor emerita at the State University of New York (SUNY). Dr. Hammond has held the following positions: chair of educational administration at SUNY New Paltz, principal and business administrator at Tuxedo, New York; high school music director at North Salem, New York, and sixth grade teacher at Phoenix, New York. She has written and presented at national conferences on motivation, teacher leadership, competitive advantage for schools, and the importance of board retreats and the superintendency. She has held the positions of NYS ASCD president, ASCD Affiliate Board, ASCD Technology liaison to aol.com, and numerous other state leadership positions. Dr. Hammond has a bachelor of science from State University of New York, a master's degree in music from Western Connecticut State University, a master's in educational leadership from the Southern Connecticut State University, and a doctorate in educational administration from Teachers College, Columbia University.

Rita Senor is an author, a consultant on leadership and motivation, and is recognized for creating quality school cultures. As a retired administrator and teacher from New York State, Ms. Senor has taught academics and the fine arts for all grade levels. She has held positions of middle and high school principal, central office curriculum leader, adjunct professor in educational leadership, and orchestra conductor. She has a bachelor of science from Boston University, a master's degree in music education from Western Connecticut State University, a master's degree in elementary education and a master's degree in educational administration from State University of New York at New Paltz.